GEORGE
W.BUSH

Look for more fascinating biographies in the series!

Barack Obama

Steve Jobs

Nelson Mandela

Sally Ride

A REAL-LIFE STORY

GEORGE
W. BUSH

OUR FORTY-THIRD PRESIDENT

Previously titled
President George W. Bush: Our Forty-Third President

by BEATRICE GORMLEY

ALADDIN

New York   London   Toronto   Sydney   New Delhi

ALADDIN

An imprint of Simon & Schuster Children's Publishing Division

1230 Avenue of the Americas, New York, NY 10020

This Aladdin hardcover edition September 2015

Text copyright © 2001, 2005, 2015 by Beatrice Gormley

Previously titled *President George W. Bush: Our Forty-Third President*

Front jacket photograph copyright © 2015 by Allan Tannenbaum-Pool/Getty Images

Back jacket photograph copyright © 2015 by Jim Young/Reuters/Corbis

All rights reserved, including the right of reproduction in whole or in part in any form.

ALADDIN is a trademark of Simon & Schuster, Inc., and related logo is a registered

trademark of Simon & Schuster, Inc.

For information about special discounts for bulk purchases, please contact

Simon & Schuster Special Sales at 1-866-506-1949 or business@simonandschuster.com.

The Simon & Schuster Speakers Bureau can bring authors to your live event. For more

information or to book an event contact the Simon & Schuster Speakers Bureau at

1-866-248-3049 or visit our website at www.simonspeakers.com.

Book design by Karina Granda

The text of this book was set in Bembo STD.

Manufactured in the United States of America 0815 FFG

2 4 6 8 10 9 7 5 3 1

Library of Congress Control Number 2015937915

ISBN 978-1-4814-4645-7 (hc)

ISBN 978-1-4814-4647-1 (eBook)

To my husband, Bob,
who got me interested in politics

CONTENTS

CONTENTS

GEORGE
W.BUSH

CHAPTER 1
THE FIRSTBORN SON

IN JULY 1946 GEORGE W. BUSH WENT TO HIS FIRST party. It was the lawn party after his christening in New Haven, Connecticut. He had been born only a few days before, on July 6. That made him a member of the "baby boom" generation, born after World War II.

This baby was the first child of Barbara Pierce Bush and George Herbert Walker Bush. The baby's father—tall, lean, and good-looking—was a student at Yale University. The lively, auburn-haired mother had been a student at Smith College. They named their baby George Walker Bush—not exactly George Jr., but very close. They called him Georgie.

Georgie's father would become the forty-first president of the United States, but not for another forty-two years. However, even in those early days George Bush had already given his son a great deal to live up to. At Andover, a top-rate preparatory school in Massachusetts, he had been a baseball star. In World War II he had been a navy fighter pilot, a war hero.

Both of Georgie's parents came from families who had done well in business. One of his grandfathers was a Wall Street investor, and the other was the president of a large publishing company. For generations both sides of the family had been influential in politics.

For two years after Georgie's birth the Bush family lived in a little apartment in New Haven while George finished his degree at Yale. He was a baseball star in college, as he had been in prep school. Barbara, an enthusiastic sports fan, took her little son to the games to cheer on his first-baseman father.

After George Bush graduated from Yale in 1948, he could have stepped into a comfortable job in the financial world in New York, like his father and grandfather. But George was looking for a more adventurous career, away from his father's eye. Barbara, who had grown up in the wealthy suburb of Rye, New York, encouraged her husband. She, too, was eager to get away from their families and do something different.

One of the most exciting business opportunities in the country at that time was in the oil fields of Texas. With the new technology developed during World War II, drillers could reach deeper oil deposits. And as the economy boomed, the demand for fuel was skyrocketing.

So in the summer of 1948 George Bush accepted a job in Texas. He was hired by Neil Mallon, a close family friend who headed an oil corporation. Revving the engine of his red two-door Studebaker, a graduation present from his parents, George drove all the way from the East Coast to West Texas.

A week later Barbara and Georgie flew out to Texas to join George. They found a place quite different from green, woodsy New England. Around the working-class town of Odessa the land stretched flat, bleak, and dusty all the way to the horizon. Instead of pine-scented sea breezes, there were hot winds that blew sand and tumbleweeds down the street. And when the wind blew a certain way, there was also the strong smell of oil fumes from the nearby plants.

The Bushes' living quarters were not inviting either. Despite his wealthy background, George Bush was starting at the bottom in the oil business. The Bushes' home in Odessa was a two-room apartment, and they shared a bathroom with another family. They were thankful to have a bathroom at all, though, since most of their neighbors used outhouses. And the Bushes had a refrigerator—also unusual in that neighborhood.

But West Texas was a "fabulous place," as George wrote to a friend the next year. "Fortunes can be made in the land end of the oil business, and of course can be lost." He spent long hours out in the oil fields, learning the business from the ground up.

Meanwhile, Barbara took care of Georgie and got used to living where people were "Eastern-prejudiced," as she put it in a letter to her family. She missed her old friends and family. But Barbara was naturally cheerful and good at getting along with all kinds of people, and she had unshakable faith in George. She adored their two-year-old son.

So did George. "He is really cute," Georgie's father wrote to a friend in August 1948. "Whenever I come home he greets me and talks a blue streak, sentences disjointed of course but enthusiasm and spirit boundless. He is a real blond and pot-bellied. He tries to say everything and the results are often hilarious. . . . He seems to be very happy wherever he is and he is very good about amusing himself in the small yard we have here."

George and Barbara hoped to have several children, and they were delighted when a daughter was born in December 1949. They named her Pauline Robinson Bush, after Barbara's mother, and they nicknamed her Robin. Barbara came home from the hospital with Georgie's new sister on Christmas Day. That was the same Christmas that Georgie's grandfather Pierce gave the Bushes one of those new inventions, a television set. It was a hulking thing, with a tiny yellow screen.

The following year, 1950, the Bushes bought a house in Midland, not as close to the oil fields as their first home in West Texas. The house was in a new development, nicknamed Easter Egg Row because each of the little two-bedroom houses plunked down on the dirt roads was painted a different color. Otherwise, they were all exactly the same. The Bushes' house, on East Maple (there were no actual maple trees, or any other trees), was light blue.

The Bushes' new neighborhood was full of young families from other parts of the country, all hoping to strike it rich in the oil business. George and Barbara quickly made friends, and so did Georgie. One of his first and best friends was the boy next door, Randy Roden.

Although George Bush was working as hard as ever,

he had plenty of energy left over for community life. He and Barbara led the drive to build a community theater in Midland. George and the other fathers started a Little League team, clearing tumbleweeds from the yellow sand to make a baseball diamond. Both he and Barbara taught Sunday school at the First Presbyterian Church.

Barbara also helped organize charities, volunteered at the Midland hospital, and pitched in to start a local YMCA. Among many other activities, the YMCA offered electric-train races for boys and their fathers. A few years later Georgie would get his picture in the *Midland Reporter-Telegram* for winning first place in the eight-year-old division.

Every weekend backyard barbecues filled Midland's dry air with the scent of grilled hamburgers. Friends and neighbors milled around the Bushes' backyard, while little kids ran back and forth. Georgie often wore his beloved cowboy outfit, including hat, boots, bandanna, and lasso. His sister, Robin, was beginning to walk.

Less than a year after the Bushes moved to Midland, George decided to go into the oil business for himself. He and a neighbor across the street formed a company. Now George Bush was busier than ever. But he made a point of spending time with his son, often playing catch in the backyard.

Sometimes Mr. Bush took Georgie and his friend Randy out into the oil fields with him. The oil patch, with its towering derricks, was like a strange forest in that flat, treeless country. At night oil fumes blurred the bright stars of the desert sky, and machinery clanked as the pumps worked around the clock. The boys would sleep in the back of the station wagon while George Bush checked the wells.

During the hottest part of the broiling West Texas summers George, Barbara, Georgie, and Robin took off for the cool coast of Maine. All the relatives gathered at the family retreat on Walker's Point in Kennebunkport. Sometimes the Bushes stayed with George's uncle Herbie Walker, who was backing George's business. Grandfather Prescott Bush was always there, dignified and stern—"scary," the kids of the Bush-Walker clan called him. But Grandmother Dorothy Walker Bush was kind, and great fun for sports-loving children to be with.

Dorothy "Dotty" Bush and Georgie adored each other. She was just as competitive as he was—maybe more so. There was a Bush family legend about Dotty as a young married woman: When she was nine months pregnant with George's brother Prescott Jr., she played in a family baseball game. Not only that, but she hit a home run and ran all the way around the diamond—then hastily left for the hospital to give birth.

In 1952, when Georgie was six, the Bush family moved to a three-bedroom house on Ohio Street, not far from the Midland Country Club. Here the streets were paved, and there were even a few oak trees. Georgie and Mike Proctor, his friend across the street, walked or rode their bikes to Sam Houston Elementary School.

The Bushes were still in West Texas, where sometimes tumbleweeds rolled into the yard and stuck to the screen doors, and sometimes sandstorms blew so thick that Georgie couldn't see the back fence from the window. But to Georgie these were just minor annoyances. Life was mostly wonderful, full of bike races and sleepovers with friends like Randy Roden, and stunts like hanging by his knees from the struts beneath the high school football stadium.

Nineteen fifty-two was also the year that Grandfather Prescott Bush, back in Connecticut, ran for election to the U.S. Senate. He had been defeated in the 1950 race for senator, so the Bush family were especially eager for him to win this time. They were also rooting for General Dwight "Ike" Eisenhower to win the presidential campaign for the Republicans.

George Bush organized a local Republican committee in Midland and campaigned enthusiastically for Ike. But he had to do so, he joked, "making no reference to the word *Republican*." Texas, like all Southern states, had been fiercely Democratic since the Civil War.

Dwight Eisenhower won the election, and so did Grandfather Bush. Just a few months later, in February 1953, the Bushes had a new baby, John Ellis Bush. Because of his initials, they called him Jeb or Jebby. Robin was three, growing bigger and more fun for Georgie to play with all the time—although she was still properly impressed with her big brother. George Bush's business, now named Zapata Petroleum Corporation, was going well. Everyone was happy, especially Georgie.

And then one day in March the happiness fell apart. It began with something strange, but not really frightening at first: Robin didn't bounce out of bed in the morning like her usual lively self. She told her mother her plans for the day: "I may go out and lie on the grass and watch the cars go by, or I might just stay in bed."

Her worried mother took her to the doctor, who ordered tests. The test results yielded grim news: Robin had advanced leukemia, a cancer of the bone marrow. There was no cure, the doctor explained to Robin's shocked parents. She did not have long to live.

But George and Barbara were determined not to give up hope. At least they would get the best possible medical treatment for their daughter. While friends in Midland took care of Georgie and the baby, they flew Robin to a hospital in New York.

For the next six months, Georgie's mother lived in New York most of the time, spending her days with Robin. Georgie's father shuttled between New York and Midland, tending to business and keeping an eye on Georgie and Jebby. Every morning he went by the church to pray for Robin. Grandmother Dorothy Bush helped by sending the nurse who had taken care of her boys to stay with Georgie and Jeb.

All this time Georgie knew only that his sister was in New York seeing a doctor because she was sick. When his mother brought Robin home for a brief stay, she seemed like the same old Robin: curly blond hair, funny little smile. But there were bruises on her arms and legs, and

Barbara wouldn't let Georgie wrestle with Robin the way he used to.

One day in October, Georgie was at school as usual. He was carrying a record player back to the principal's office from his second-grade classroom. He happened to be outside in a covered walkway when he saw his parents' green Oldsmobile drive up in front of the school. He was sure he glimpsed the top of Robin's head above the back-seat. Setting the record player down, he ran for the car.

But Robin wasn't in the car. And George and Barbara had to tell their son the bad news they had been holding back since March. Robin had been very, very sick, and now she had died. She was buried in Greenwich, Connecticut, where George had grown up.

"I was sad, I was stunned," George W. Bush later described his reaction. "Minutes before I had had a little sister, and now I did not." He cried; his father and mother cried. Georgie couldn't believe his parents had known for so long that Robin was dying and hadn't told him. As they drove to their friends' house to pick up Jebby, Georgie kept asking questions, although he could see how painful it was for them to explain.

The months to come were a strange period for the

energetic, upbeat Bush family. "I remember being sad," said George W. Bush. Susie Evans, a friend at Sam Houston Elementary School, remembered the same thing, "a great sadness." Georgie missed Robin terribly, and it was hard to watch his parents suffering.

In his seven-year-old way, Georgie did his best to comfort his mother and father. Instead of playing with friends, he would spend afternoons with his mother. Once, at a football game with his father, he said he wished he were Robin. George, shocked at first, asked why. "I bet she can see the game better from up there than we can here," explained Georgie. To a sports-minded boy, a good view of football plays would be one of the major advantages of being in heaven.

CHAPTER 2

BASEBALL, BUSINESS, AND POLITICS

FOR A LONG TIME AFTER ROBIN DIED, GEORGIE BUSH had nightmares. And his mother's glossy auburn hair started turning gray that year, though she was only twenty-eight. The Bush family would never be quite the same.

But gradually the sad time became part of the past. Grandfather and Grandmother Bush gave them a portrait of Robin, and it was hung in the dining room. Georgie and his family began enjoying the many good things in their life again—their friends in Midland, all the oil flowing from the Zapata Petroleum Corporation wells, the new collie puppy.

The puppy, Mark, was given to the Bushes by a friend during Robin's illness. He grew up as one of the family. Some mornings the collie would follow Georgie to school. He'd have to run home with the dog and then dash back to school just before the bell.

The Ohio Street neighborhood was swarming with children, and Georgie was the leader of the pack. With many of the fathers, including George Bush, away much of the time on business, the mothers all looked out for one another's children. Barbara Bush, friendly and frank and quick with a funny remark, was a favorite with the neighborhood kids. One of Georgie's friends, Terry Throckmorton, described later how he felt about Mrs. Bush: "If I had to go talk to somebody about my troubles, it would have been her."

West Texas public schools weren't especially good, but Georgie's school was one of the better ones. The parents of the students at Sam Houston Elementary School were well educated, and they saw to it that their children did their homework. George and Barbara Bush were leaders of a drive to build a library for the school. One year they were cochairs of the Midland PTA.

At school Georgie dressed in a white T-shirt and blue jeans like the other boys. He was intelligent but not at all bookish. In fact, he could be a rascal. Georgie's third-grade teacher, Austine Crosby, remembered one day of inside recess when he threw a football through a window.

Like his mother, Georgie was quick with a smart

remark, and the other children thought of him as a wise guy. One time he entertained his fourth-grade classmates by drawing an ink mustache, goatee, and sideburns on himself. The teacher marched Georgie to the principal, who gave him three spanks with a paddle.

In the spring Georgie and his friends would hurry to school—to play pickup baseball before classes began. The principal would take his coat off and bat some balls for the boys to field. Like most people in Midland, the principal believed that sports were important. When the World Series was going on, Georgie and his classmates were allowed to watch the games during rest period.

This focus on sports seemed natural to Georgie. All the Bushes, including the relatives back East, loved sports—baseball, football, tennis, golf. They watched and played the games enthusiastically. On visits with his grandparents back East, Georgie was taught by his uncle Bucky to root for baseball's New York Giants. "To this day," says George W. Bush with a touch of pride, "I can recite the starting lineup of the 1954 Giants team. Willie Mays was my hero."

Sometimes Grandfather and Grandmother Bush came to visit Midland. The Bushes' friends were greatly impressed to rub shoulders with a U.S. senator. But they were also nervous, because Senator Bush was so formal in his clothes and manner.

Once, George Bush flew Georgie and his friend Randy Roden to Washington, D.C., where they had lunch at the older Bushes' townhouse. Georgie was used to his grand-parents' lifestyle, and he knew that you were supposed to dip your fingers politely in the glass bowl in front of your place at the table. But Randy had never seen a finger bowl before. To the Bushes' surprise, he drank the water from it.

Georgie was unaware, of course, of another man in Washington who had been elected to the Senate at the same time as Grandfather Bush. This man, Senator Albert Gore Sr., had a son, Al, two years younger than Georgie. Almost fifty years later George W. Bush and Al Gore would face each other as rivals for the highest office in the land.

By 1955, when Georgie was nine, George Bush's oil busi-ness was doing better than ever. The family could move to an even bigger house in Midland. They needed more room because they had another new baby, "our third giant boy," as George Bush jokingly put it. They named him Neil Mallon Bush, after the family friend who had helped George get started in the oil business. Later, in 1956, they had another boy, named Marvin Pierce Bush after Barbara's father.

Barbara had two black maids, Julia May Cooper and Otha Taylor, to help her with the big house and family. There weren't many black people in Midland, but the town, like the rest of the South, was nonetheless racially segregated in those days. In the county courthouse there were separate drinking fountains and restrooms, labeled WHITE and COLORED. The Midland bus station had two separate waiting rooms. Neighborhoods and schools were segregated too, by an unwritten code that kept Latino and African-American families separate from white families.

Georgie's friend Mike Proctor remembered the first time he had an inkling that racial slurs were wrong. It was the time when Georgie, about eight, came out with an expression insulting to black people in front of his mother. Many of the kids at Sam Houston Elementary School used this expression all the time, and Mike thought nothing of it. To his surprise, Barbara Bush dragged her son into the bathroom, washed his mouth out with soap, and gave him a stern lecture.

The Bushes' roomy brick ranch house had a swimming pool, and it backed up to the grassy stretches of McCall Park. All the kids in the neighborhood seemed to be based at the Bushes', with Mark, the Bushes' collie, running back and forth among them. Before long the collie was joined by a new puppy, Nicky, a poodle mix who grew up to look like a lamb.

Georgie was six and a half years older than Jeb, the next-oldest boy in the Bush family. He was too old to spend much time with his little brothers. When Georgie and his friends weren't playing baseball at the park, they might play sandlot football, or ride their bikes downtown to see a movie.

In April 1955 Georgie's father wrote to his grandfather Pierce, "He is out for Little League—so eager. He tries so very hard. It makes me think back to all the times I tried out, etc. He has good fast hands and even seems to be able to hit a little. I get as much kick out of watching him trying out as I do out of all our varied business efforts."

To Georgie's and his father's satisfaction, he made the Little League team, the Midland Cubs. For the next several years he spent every possible minute playing baseball. Georgie had been working up to this ever since he was a toddler in Connecticut, watching his father play baseball for Yale. Now his one ambition was to become a Major League Baseball player. Scrappy and fearless, Georgie usually played the position of catcher.

When George Bush was home, he would join Georgie and his friends for practice in the park. They begged him to demonstrate his neat trick of catching fly balls behind his back. Joe O'Neill, one of Georgie's Little League teammates, once went home with his baseball cap sticking to the scrapes on his scalp. He had been trying, not very successfully, to imitate Mr. Bush.

Georgie had an excellent memory, although he didn't necessarily apply it at school. He put this talent to use memorizing the statistics of his idol Willie Mays, star slugger and center fielder for the Giants. He memorized the stats of *all* the Major League Baseball players. His father encouraged him, drilling Georgie and his friends from his large collection of baseball cards.

Georgie soon had his own shoe box full of cards, and he and his friends traded cards and discussed the players and the games endlessly. Terry Throckmorton, whose father was the head of Midland Little League, remembered later how he and Georgie would send baseball cards to the players and ask for their autograph. Willie Mays and Mickey Mantle were among the famous players who signed Georgie's cards and sent them back.

Although Georgie's father was often away on business,

the father and son spent some special times together. In March 1956 Mr. Bush's company launched a powerful new high-tech oil rig in Galveston, on the coast of Texas. Almost ten, Georgie stood proudly on the deck of the oil platform beside his father, each of them dressed in a suit with a white carnation in the lapel. In August 1957, when Georgie was eleven, he was the only one of the Bush children to fly to the family retreat in Kennebunkport with his father. Barbara and the three younger children made the long drive to Maine in the car with the two maids, Julia May and Otha.

In the fall of 1958 Georgie began the seventh grade at San Jacinto Junior High School. There he won his first election, to the office of class president. He also played football, a big deal in Midland even in seventh grade. Barbara Bush came to every game to support Georgie's team.

Years later George W. Bush would describe his childhood in Midland as "a happy blur," "surrounded by love and friends and sports."

By the end of 1958 George Bush's oil business had shifted to Houston, on the Gulf of Mexico, three hundred miles from Midland. The Bushes would have to move. In the spring of 1959 Mr. and Mrs. Bush left for Houston.

The boys stayed behind in Midland with a sitter, to finish out the school year.

Shortly after Georgie and his brothers joined their parents in Houston, one more baby was born to George and Barbara Bush. This time it was a girl. They named her Dorothy Walker Bush, after George's mother, and they called her Doro.

Houston was then the largest city in Texas, much bigger than Midland. It was damp and green in contrast to dry, brown Midland. The Bush family had a nice new house, complete with swimming pool and their own baseball field.

All the Bushes had been sorry to leave their good friends and close community in Midland. But they quickly made new friends in Houston. Georgie easily fit into his eighth-grade class at the Kincaid School, one of the most exclusive private schools in Texas. Good-looking, outgoing, and good at sports, he was elected a class officer.

At home, as the oldest child by almost seven years, Georgie felt close to his mother. And she greatly appreciated his company, with his father away so much of the time. The oil business now took George Bush all over the world—to England, Borneo, Mexico, Kuwait.

Meanwhile, Barbara managed the family of five children with a firm hand. She was the parent who broke up fights and enforced rules such as bedtimes, curfews, and acceptable table manners.

Whether George Bush was out of town or at home, the Bushes were just as social as ever. Some of their socializing involved fund-raisers or other events for the Republican Party, which was stronger in Houston than in West Texas. The Bushes were committed to the Republicans, but they were also working toward a goal for George Bush. For a long time the idea of running for public office had been simmering in the back of his mind.

Georgie wasn't thinking of a future in politics for himself, but he could work a party like an experienced politician. A good friend of Georgie's was struck by his behavior at the barbecues and other parties. Georgie was only a young teenager like his friend, but he would greet each person in the room when he came in and say good-bye to each person when he left. He would remember each person's name, even if he had never met him or her before.

Georgie had seen his father socialize this way many times, of course. But he also had his own natural ability to connect with people. "His father had a definite influence on him," commented his history teacher at Kincaid. "But his general relationship to people was more like his mother's. He was very intense."

Up to this point, Georgie's childhood in Texas had been very different from his father's childhood in New England. But now his mother and father began to explain that they wanted him to go to Phillips Academy, in Andover, Massachusetts. They felt that it would be good for their son to live on his own, away from the family.

Since the time Georgie was born, his family had expected that he would follow in his father's footsteps to Andover and then to Yale University. Academically, Andover was far above Kincaid. In fact, it was one of the best schools in the country. Andover had a long, awe-inspiring tradition, including the time George Washington himself addressed the students from horseback.

One afternoon in the spring of 1961, when George W. Bush was fourteen, his mother greeted him with, "Congratulations, George!" His acceptance had come, and he would leave for Andover in the fall.

CHAPTER 3

ANDOVER

FOR GEORGE BUSH, GROWING UP IN CONNECTICUT in the 1930s and 1940s, New England had been home. But for his son George W. Bush in the fall of 1961, it was a cold, strange land. And Andover itself was a shock to George W.'s system. There were no girls. The dormitories were poorly heated. The younger boys were not allowed to have radios.

The headmaster, John Mason Kemper, was a proud graduate of West Point. He ran the school with strict discipline and high standards. Life at Andover was a continual round of classes, athletics, required daily chapel attendance—and very little free time. Lights had to be off at 10:00 P.M.

Part of the Andover discipline was the dress code. Jacket and tie were required in chapel, in classes, and at

24

meals. George, an informal Texan and not naturally tidy, pushed the code as far as he could. With the jacket he'd wear a wrinkled shirt, or sneakers with no socks, and his tie would be carelessly knotted. The jacket might even be an army surplus jacket.

In the classroom the competition was fierce. George was used to competition in sports, and he enjoyed it. But he was also used to getting A's in his classes without trying. At the beginning of his first year at Andover, George was seriously worried about flunking out and disgracing himself and his family.

It was a nasty shock when George received a "big fat zero" on his first English composition. The subject of his essay was his sister Robin's death. As he worked on the paper he decided he'd used the word *tears* (though they *had* cried a lot of tears) too many times. George looked in his thesaurus and found an impressive-looking substitute word: *lacrimates*. But George's English teacher was not impressed, or even touched by the story of Robin's death. "Disgraceful," he scrawled across the paper in red ink.

Adding to the pressure on George W., his father was a legend at the school. Many teachers still thought of George Bush the elder as the ideal Andover student. He'd had excellent grades and had also been captain of the varsity baseball and soccer teams and president of the senior class. His yearbook title of "Best All-around Fellow" summed it up.

Also, George W.'s father was admired because he had signed up to fight in World War II right after graduating from Andover. Japan had bombed Pearl Harbor in December 1941, the year George H. W. Bush was a senior. His father, Prescott Bush, tried to convince him to go on to Yale first. But George enlisted—and became a war hero.

Fortunately for George W.'s morale that first year at Andover, there were a few other boys with Texan accents in his class. One of them was Randy Roden, his old friend from the earliest days in Midland. Another was Clay Johnson from Fort Worth, who became a lifelong good friend. John Kidde, a blond surfer from California, and Rob Dieter, a football player from Florida, also gravitated to George's group.

George W. played junior varsity basketball and baseball his first year, and he joined the Spanish Club. He was only moderately good at sports, for an Andover athlete. But he was always happy and comfortable on a team. In the high-ceilinged, dark-paneled dining hall the boys could choose where to sit, and they grouped themselves into the serious students and the jocks, or athletes. George and his friends sat at the jocks' end of the room.

Even the New England winters couldn't dampen George W.'s bouncy spirits. At the first snowfall in October he dashed outside and frolicked like a puppy. "Look at the snow!" The boys from the Northeast were embarrassed for him, but he didn't care. He caught snowflakes on his tongue and tried to scrape together enough for a snowball.

Although George W.'s grandfather was a U.S. senator, George never tried to impress his classmates with this fact. Many of them had no idea who his grandfather was. José Gonzalez, a boy from Puerto Rico, was once invited by George to his grandparents' in Connecticut for Thanksgiving. He was surprised to hear other people address Prescott Bush as "Senator."

During the early 1960s the civil rights movement was gathering strength, and the Cold War between the United States and the Soviet Union was heating up. The Cold War came to a crisis in October 1962, when President John F. Kennedy threatened Premier Nikita Khrushchev with nuclear war over Soviet missiles in Cuba. That same month, President Kennedy sent federal troops to the

University of Mississippi to force the school to admit black students.

But George W. didn't pay much attention to such world-shaking events. At Andover the big news in October 1962 was that Headmaster Kemper was on the cover of *Time* magazine. EXCELLENCE AND INTENSITY IN U.S. PREP SCHOOLS, read the headline. George himself wanted to be excellent and intense, but not exactly the way that Kemper meant. And different from the way people remembered his father.

One thing George excelled in was getting people to laugh. His friend Donald E. Vermeil (George nicknamed him "Vermin") remembered junior year, when they roomed together, as "probably the funniest year of my life." George, said Vermeil, "had a way of keeping everything light and entertaining without offending people or getting out of line." For his witty remarks George was nicknamed "Lip."

Meanwhile, back in Houston, George's father was making his move into politics. He had been thinking about running for office for some time. He believed deeply in Prescott Bush's idea that people who had the money and ability also had a duty to serve in the government. In March 1963 George Bush was elected chairman of the Republican Party in Harris County, Texas.

George W. didn't pay much attention to political issues. But because of his grandfather, Senator Prescott Bush, he was used to hearing about the different personalities in Washington. George's friend John Kidde, invited to a Bush family Thanksgiving in Connecticut, was impressed that George could follow the senator's conversation about Washington politics. George might not know the pros and cons of a political argument, but he knew who the politicians were. It was like following the New York Yankees baseball team—the important thing was to know the players.

In September 1963 George's father announced that *he* was becoming a player in the political game. He would run for the U.S. Senate next year. He was also enthusiastic about Senator Barry Goldwater of Arizona as a Republican candidate for president in 1964. That October, Senator Goldwater visited Andover and spoke to the students.

Later, John Kidde was surprised to see Goldwater's book *The Conscience of a Conservative* lying on George W.'s desk. Andover students had heavy reading assignments for their classes, and it was unusual for them to read books on their own. But George explained that his parents had given him Goldwater's book. George read the book because his father thought it was important.

On November 22, 1963, President John F. Kennedy was assassinated in Dallas. Like the rest of the country, Andover students were deeply shaken. That night George and his roommate, John Kidde, stayed up late talking. George "was very upset about the tragedy," said John. He sensed a difference in the way George thought about the assassination. Whereas John was stunned that the president of the country had been shot, George thought of it more as the death of a real person. To George, John F. Kennedy was one of the players in his grandfather's political game.

During his four years at Andover, George W. gradually carved his own niche. He couldn't be the most brilliant student on campus, or an outstanding athlete, as his father had been. But he was one of the friendliest, most enthusiastic boys at the school.

George W.'s enthusiasm was contagious, and he had a way of getting people to do things. Senior year he was chosen as head cheerleader of the squad of nine. Their role was to whip up school spirit for the Andover-Exeter football games. "Group guts! Group guts!" George would get the whole school chanting at pep rallies.

George worked up a series of humorous skits for assemblies. In one of these skits he and the other cheerleaders dressed up like girls, in wigs and short white skirts. The dean of students, G. Grenville Benedict, later said that George had raised school spirit at Andover to its highest level in many years.

Andover was an all-male school, and the social life there was almost nonexistent. The pressure to excel in academics and sports didn't leave much time for dating. For the older boys there were a few awkward afternoon dances with local girls' schools.

George did manage to find a girl he liked the summer between his junior and senior year. They were both vacationing in Kennebunkport, and they met on the beach. Debbie Taylor, a pretty, lively Californian, happened to know George's friend John Kidde. After dating Debbie a few times during a visit with John in California, George invited her to the prom in May of his senior year. They had a good time together, but neither of them was serious about the other.

During the spring of his senior year George and his classmates suffered under the pressure to get into topflight colleges. George had applied to Yale, of course, since his whole family expected him to go there. But he wasn't sure he would be accepted. He tried to talk as if he'd be just as happy to go to the University of Texas, his "safety school."

At the height of this almost unbearable tension George appeared at a school assembly wearing a top hat and sunglasses. He gravely announced the formation of an intramural stickball league, with himself as "high commissioner." The audience roared with laughter—and they eagerly signed up for the stickball tournament.

Stickball, played with a broomstick and a tennis ball, was quite a departure from serious Andover athletics. Each dormitory had at least one team, with names like the Steamers and the Beavers. The players printed their nicknames—"Vermin," "McScuz"—on their T-shirts. With much pomp and fuss, George laid down the rules of the sport and gave out decisions. "Stickball was a way to . . . let off some of the inevitable senior year springtime steam," explained one of George's classmates.

In the 1964 Andover yearbook George won the title of "Big Man on Campus." But he was *not* called "Most Likely to Succeed." Years later, during the presidential race of 2000, one of George's classmates was asked what the boys at Andover thought of George W. in 1964. What if someone had predicted that George would be a candidate for president one day? "The reaction," the classmate answered, "would have been gales of laughter."

When George W.'s acceptance from Yale arrived that spring, he was giddy with relief. He would be one of thirty in his Andover class to attend Yale University.

So George would follow his father and his grandfather to Yale. But first he returned to Houston to join his father's campaign for the U.S. Senate.

CHAPTER 4
FATHER-SON CAMPAIGNING

GEORGE W. BUSH'S GRANDFATHER PRESCOTT BUSH had decided not to run for reelection in 1962, so there was no longer a Bush in national office. It was time for the next generation to step up to the plate.

After his graduation from Andover, George W. flew straight home to Houston. His father had won the Republican primary on June 6. Now his campaign against his Democratic opponent, Ralph Yarborough, was in full swing. George W.'s brothers were too young to campaign, but the eldest son could be a real asset to his father.

It would be a tough race, because the Democratic candidate had all the backing of President Lyndon B. Johnson. President Johnson, a Texan and formerly the Democratic majority leader of the Senate, was enormously popular in the state. He had grown up in the hill country of West

Texas, and he knew how to remind the voters that he was a "good ol' boy." That spring he had been the graduation speaker at the same small-town high school from which he graduated in 1924.

President Johnson had an ambitious plan for the country, a "war on poverty." This series of programs would, among other things, improve education in poor neighborhoods, fight crime in urban areas, and fund health care for senior citizens. Many conservatives thought Johnson's plan for a "Great Society" was too costly. They worried that the government would have to raise taxes in order to pay for Johnson's new programs.

George Bush, squarely opposing Johnson's program, had the backing of businessmen in Houston. But in the rest of Texas he was hardly even known. He was determined to change that by speaking to voters all across the state. He wrote to a friend, "Campaigning in Texas on a statewide basis is more exhausting than anything I have done."

In the sweltering heat of July candidate George Bush hit the campaign trail again in a bus dubbed the Bush Bandwagon. Barbara and George W. rode with him. They planned to visit forty cities across the huge state of Texas.

At every appearance a country-and-western group, the Black Mountain Boys, would warm up the crowd. A group of Republican women, the Bush Bluebonnet Belles, sang a campaign song:

> The sun's going to shine in the Senate someday.
> George Bush is going to chase them liberals away.

In town after dusty town, at women's coffees and neighborhood barbecues, candidate George Bush explained his positions. They were very much like the positions of presidential candidate Barry Goldwater. He was against President Johnson's civil rights bill. He was for the war in Vietnam. He opposed "wildly spending money on antipoverty programs," as he called the president's "War on Poverty."

George W. had just turned eighteen, but he impressed many people on his father's campaign. Part of his role in the campaign, of course, was just to stand up in front of audiences, as living proof that his father was a family man. But young George also caught on to politics quickly. While he was outgoing and pleasant to everyone, he understood that it was important to be discreet. He didn't talk about the campaign outside the inner circle.

In September, George left the campaign to start his freshman year at Yale. He was rooming with Clay Johnson and Rob Dieter, both friends from Andover.

At Yale, as at Andover, George W. felt pressure to live up to his father's achievements. George H. W. Bush had been a baseball star at Yale—there was a picture of him standing beside visiting baseball legend Babe Ruth. His good grades had gotten him into Phi Beta Kappa, the honor society. He had been president of his fraternity, Delta Kappa Epsilon. He had been invited into the highly regarded secret society Skull and Bones.

George W. couldn't match his father's record at Yale any more than he had at Andover. But he had his own unique talents. His roommates were impressed with his behavior during the first week of freshman year. While many freshmen were busy setting up their rooms or worrying about their classes, George went out and met people. "Within three to four days," said Dieter, "a big percent of the people knew who he was."

In 1964 political awareness was high at Yale, and it was taking a turn in the liberal direction. Most students favored Lyndon Johnson over Barry Goldwater for president that fall. There was increasing concern about the threat of nuclear war, and Senator Goldwater seemed to favor the use of nuclear weapons. And Goldwater opposed civil rights legislation, which Yale students tended to support.

Students were also worried about the growing war in Vietnam, although President Johnson had promised not to widen the conflict. In August the president had pushed the Gulf of Tonkin Resolution through Congress. This act gave the president the power to wage war in Vietnam, even though Congress had not declared war.

Just before election day at the beginning of November, George W. left Yale for Houston. He wanted to be with his father on election night. George Bush's Democratic opponent, Ralph Yarborough, had run a mean campaign, and it looked as if he would win.

Yarborough had accused George Bush of being a carpetbagger—not a real Texan, but a society Easterner. George Bush tried to turn the *carpetbagger* term into a joke. "I *would* have been born in Texas," he retorted, "but I wanted to be close to my mother."

On election night at the Bush headquarters in Hotel America, George W.'s job was to put the election results up on the board. It was discouraging work. Bush had done well for a Republican in Texas—but not nearly well enough to win. Senator Barry Goldwater, too, lost to President Lyndon Johnson by a landslide. Besides his own state of Arizona, the only states Goldwater carried were five Deep South states where racial tensions were high.

Before midnight George Bush had to concede the election to Ralph Yarborough. Barbara and George W. stood beside him at that painful moment. "I guess I have a lot to learn about politics," said Bush to the press. Later, in private, Barbara cried openly, and George W. had tears in his eyes.

When George W. returned to Yale, everyone knew about his father's defeat. Since Bush was a Yale graduate, the *Yale Daily News* had featured a story about him on election day. In mock elections held earlier that fall, the students had voted for Yarborough by a small margin.

Crossing the campus shortly after the election, George W. happened to see the Reverend William Sloane Coffin Jr., the chaplain at Yale. Coffin was a supporter of peace movements at Yale, and he would become famous for his stand against the Vietnam War and for civil rights. He was politically liberal, and was becoming more so all the time.

But to George, political issues were much less important than knowing who your friends were. The main thing

George knew about Coffin was that he had gone to Yale with his father after World War II, and that they had both been in the secret society Skull and Bones. By Bush family standards, that meant that Coffin must be a friend.

But when George W. introduced himself, he was stunned and angry at what he heard Coffin say: "Oh, yes, I know your father. Frankly, he was beaten by a better man."

A better man! In the first place, there was no better man in the *world* than George H. W. Bush, as far as his son was concerned. And how could Reverend Coffin say something so unkind to George W.? His father had just worked his heart out in a campaign and lost.

For years afterward, George W. thought of William Sloane Coffin Jr. as typical of Eastern intellectuals. (Coffin finally heard about George's story and wrote him an apology, although he said he didn't remember making the remark.) "What angered me," said George W., "was the way such people at Yale felt so intellectually superior and so righteous. They thought they had all the answers."

CHAPTER 5

OUT OF PLACE AT YALE

DURING THE SUMMER OF 1965 GEORGE W. BUSH went to work for a drilling company in southern Louisiana. He was a roughneck, a member of the crew on an off-shore oil rig. "It was hard, hot work," he said. "I unloaded enough of those heavy mud sacks to know that was *not* what I wanted to do with my life."

George W.'s father had arranged this job so that his son could get experience in the oil business, just as he had. George W. was supposed to work there all summer, but he quit a week early. He wanted to spend more time in Houston with his Texas friends before he went back to Yale.

When his father heard what George W. had done, he called him to his office in Houston. "You agreed to work a certain amount of time, and you didn't," said George Bush. "I just want you to know that you have disappointed me."

That was the worst punishment George W. could imagine. He had disappointed his *father,* the man he admired most in the world. He said later, "When you love a person and he loves you, those are the harshest words someone can utter. I left that office realizing I had made a mistake."

George Bush made another deep impression on his son that year. Only a year earlier, Bush had been soundly defeated in the race for senator. But now he was planning to run again in 1966, this time for the U.S. House of Representatives. As George W. explained it to a friend, "This is what you do, you bounce back. So you're down, you just get back up."

Back at Yale in the fall of 1965 many students were consumed with the political issues of the day. That summer a peaceful march for voter registration in Selma, Alabama, had been attacked by state troopers with whips and tear gas. In August, Congress had passed the Voting Rights Act to guarantee black citizens the right to vote. Also, the war in Vietnam continued to grow. The United States had been bombing North Vietnam full force since the spring. U.S. soldiers, more than 180,000 of them, poured into Vietnam.

At Yale, George W. could have taken part in some fierce debates on these issues. He could have joined the Young Republicans on campus, or other Republican groups.

But although his father was steeped in political matters, George W. was not. As he explained later, his family never sat around the dinner table discussing the issues of the day. George and his brothers were much more likely to watch Marvin finish his vegetables so they all could have dessert.

Instead of getting involved in campus politics, George and his roommates pledged the Delta Kappa Epsilon fraternity. This had been his father's fraternity, which in itself was a good reason to join. Besides, the "Dekes," with their focus on sports and parties, suited George perfectly.

First, though, the pledges had to go through the humiliating hazing process. One of the ways the fraternity members tried to embarrass the pledges was to make them name all the other pledges in the room. Most of them, including George's roommate Clay Johnson, couldn't name more than four or five. But for George this challenge was easy. He had a natural interest in people, and he had an excellent memory. He rattled off the names of all fifty-four people in the room.

At Andover, George had taken an interest in history, and history would become his major at Yale. He kept up a C average, but what he was learning in class wasn't his main focus. Sports, parties, all-night card games—any activity that involved being with other people was important to him.

During the summer of 1966 George W. worked as a salesman in the sporting goods department of Sears in Houston. He liked this job, and he was naturally good at connecting with people and convincing them to buy. On his time off he began to pay a lot of attention to one particular girl, Cathryn Wolfman.

Cathryn lived in the Bushes' neighborhood in Houston, and she went to Smith College in Massachusetts. Friendly, sociable George never had any trouble getting dates, but Cathryn was much more than a date to him. She was dazzling—popular, witty, attractive, athletic, and from a cultured family.

Meanwhile, the elder George Bush's campaign for U.S. representative was under way. Bush's hard work to build up the Republican Party in Houston was paying off. Also, Jimmy Allison, a wealthy newspaper publisher and friend from Midland, was helping to run his campaign. They launched a media blitz to make sure that every single voter in the district knew who Bush was.

The Bushes' house in Houston was campaign headquarters, and the whole family was involved. On George W.'s twentieth birthday in July, the Bush campaign aired an

44

advertisement that featured the candidate and his family. The ad showed George Bush calling, "Okay, gang—pile in!" Then the Bush children ran one at a time to jump into a convertible, the Bush Bandwagon.

That fall George W. was elected president of Delta Kappa Epsilon. His fraternity brothers agreed he was the perfect person for the job. The purpose of the Dekes was socializing, and George was often the life of the party.

In the late 1940s, when George H. W. Bush went to Yale, the fraternities had been an important and respected part of life on campus. But by 1966 most students at Yale, especially the younger students, were not impressed by fraternities. The mood on many college campuses was for students to question their parents' values. If Dad had been a fraternity man, that was a reason *not* to join.

George W. couldn't understand this point of view. His family, his parents, mattered more to him than anything else. In November he flew back to Houston for election day. Again he took up his post at the tally board to write down the election results as they came in.

This year it was a happier job. Bush's tireless door-to-door campaigning had paid off. The Bush campaign's media blitz had also helped the people get to know George H. W. Bush.

The voters liked his friendly, sincere style, and they were convinced that he would work hard for them.

The numbers George W. posted on the board quickly showed that his father had won election to the House of Representatives. Bush supporters cheered and cried with joy and hugged one another. In Connecticut the candidate's parents, former senator Prescott Bush and Dorothy Walker Bush, glowed with satisfaction. Congressman George Bush would be moving to Washington in the spring. Once again there would be a Bush in national office.

Just before Christmas break George W. and some of his fraternity brothers had a run-in with the police. Wandering around New Haven, George had tried to steal a Christmas wreath from the front of a store. His idea—not very well thought out—was to take it back to the Deke house as a decoration.

Unfortunately, some police were watching from a patrol car, and they arrested George and charged him with disorderly conduct. But they didn't take the theft seriously, and the charges were dropped. George and his friends had been laughing and making a lot of noise—it was clearly a college prank.

Over Christmas break in Houston, George asked Cathryn Wolfman to marry him, and she accepted. Their engagement was announced on New Year's Day, 1967. They didn't set a definite wedding date, but they planned to get married and live together during George's last year at Yale.

George's parents may have thought he was too young to be engaged, but they liked Cathryn very much. Besides, they had gotten engaged at the same age themselves. Here again, George W. was following in his father's footsteps.

That spring George W. was invited into Skull and Bones, the most exclusive of the secret societies at Yale. His father had been a member of Skull and Bones, and so had his grandfather as well as other relatives and close family friends. Chaplain William Sloane Coffin Jr. had been in Skull and Bones the same year as the older George Bush. Now, however, Chaplain Coffin made slighting remarks about secret societies to the *New York Times*.

During George W.'s last year at Yale the Vietnam War was hard to ignore. President Johnson had sent half a million U.S. soldiers to the war. On the TV evening news, newscasters read the body count, the number of American soldiers who had been killed.

In 1967 Yale was still all male, and students worried

about being drafted as soon as they left college. At the same time, they felt guilty that so many boys their age who were not college students had already been drafted for the war. Some of those boys were dying. Most students at Yale believed that the United States should not even be in the war in Southeast Asia. Chaplain William Sloane Coffin led students in protests against the draft.

For the most part, George W. and his friends at the Deke house did not discuss the war. George played rugby, a sport he loved for its "speed and hard knocks." He attended his twice-a-week Skull and Bones meetings.

As the Deke fraternity president, George W. was called upon to defend the custom of hazing pledges. In November 1967 the *Yale Daily News* attacked fraternities, especially Deke, for hazing. The article described the ritual of branding each pledge on his back with the Delta insignia.

The story was picked up by the *New York Times,* quoting "George Bush, a Yale senior." George W. had tried to explain to the reporter that the burns from the branding were very minor, and the pledges didn't really suffer from pain. He thought everyone should understand that the hazing was just a normal part of fraternity rituals. But the mood of the late 1960s was not sympathetic to these time-honored traditions. The Yale fraternity board, after an investigation, decided to fine Deke.

Shortly afterward George had his second run-in with the police. He was in Princeton, New Jersey, for the big Ivy League championship football game between the Yale Bulldogs and the Princeton Tigers. Two of his fraternity brothers were on the football team. When Yale won, 29–7, George was in the midst of the wild crowd of Yalies who tore down the goalposts. He was sitting on the crossbar when the Princeton police showed up. They didn't actually arrest him, but they told him to leave the campus—within ten minutes—and never come back.

George W. could be wild, but not in any way that challenged "the Establishment." The Establishment was what protesters in the late 1960s called the government, businesses, parents— anyone in authority. George didn't take drugs, wear his hair long, or take part in antiwar protests. He was not a hippie.

To George, the Establishment was his father—his whole family. He might do things to annoy them, but he would never really rebel against them or question their values.

CHAPTER 6

TEXAS AIR NATIONAL GUARD

MANY STUDENTS IN GEORGE W. BUSH'S GRADU-
ating class at Yale were determined not to go to Vietnam,
and they worried about how to get out of military service.
They could enroll in divinity school, which was exempt
from the draft. They could join the Peace Corps. They
could trick the draft board into believing that they were
medically unable to serve. Or they could flee across the
U.S. border to Canada.

But it never occurred to George to try to avoid military service. Military service was a proud tradition in his
family, and his own father was a war hero. He had seen the
pictures of his father's rescue by a submarine after he was
shot down over the Pacific Ocean. Barbara Bush had glued
into a family scrapbook a small piece of the rubber life raft
that had kept her husband afloat.

George liked the idea of learning to fly a fighter plane, as his father had done. During Christmas break of his last year at Yale he applied for the Texas Air National Guard. In the National Guard he could work out his military service, but it was very unlikely that he would be sent to Vietnam.

At the same time that his son was signing up for the National Guard, Congressman Bush visited Vietnam on a congressional fact-finding mission. Bush believed the war in Vietnam was necessary in order to stop world Communism, and the visit didn't change his mind. But he did conclude that there were too many American soldiers—hundreds of thousands now—in Vietnam.

Congressman Bush was especially disturbed that so many of the combat troops were African-American. These black men were fighting for our country. Yet back home, George Bush knew, they didn't have the same chances as white men to go to a good school or buy a house.

The spring of 1968, said George W. Bush later, "was a confusing and disturbing time." At the end of March, President Lyndon Johnson announced that he would not run for reelection. Also, he would stop the bombing of North Vietnam.

A few days after President Johnson's announcement

Dr. Martin Luther King Jr., an esteemed African-American activist, was assassinated in Memphis, Tennessee. There were riots in Washington, D.C., where George W.'s parents, brothers, and sister had moved the previous spring. Barbara Bush saw the smoke rising from burning buildings just a few blocks from their house.

Four days before George W.'s graduation in June another assassination shocked the country. Robert Kennedy, brother of the late President John F. Kennedy and now candidate for president himself, was shot in California. George and his friends listened to the radio reports in stunned disbelief.

To add to the strangeness of that graduation, Yale chaplain William Sloane Coffin was not present. He was in Boston, on trial for helping students resist the military draft. At Yale the class of 1968 passed around a petition against the war in Vietnam. Most of the class signed it, but not George or his friends.

George W.'s father came to his son's graduation, but only briefly. George W. spent most of that weekend with his friend Clay Johnson's family. "My father doesn't have a normal life," he explained.

Congressman Bush was caught up in the turmoil convulsing the country. He was a committed Republican, but he wasn't nearly as conservative as most of the voters in his district. In April, remembering the African-American soldiers he had talked with in Vietnam, he had voted for the Open Housing Bill. "Were we supposed to tell these black soldiers when they came home that they couldn't buy houses in our neighborhood?" he wondered. The voters in Bush's district in Houston were furious with him, and he received hate mail and death threats.

Congressman Bush was also caught up in the politics of that presidential election year. Now that President Johnson had decided not to run, it looked as if a Republican would have a good chance. George Bush was an enthusiastic worker for Richard Nixon, who won the Republican nomination. There was even talk that summer that Nixon might pick Congressman George Bush for his vice president.

After his graduation, George W. returned home to Houston. There Cathryn Wolfman told him that she wanted to put off their wedding plans again. They didn't break off the engagement, but gradually they drifted apart. In late July, George left for basic training at Lackland Air Force Base in San Antonio. Cathryn left for a job in

Washington, D.C. By next spring she would be married to someone else.

Politically, things were going the way the Bushes felt they ought to go. After a close contest Richard Nixon had been elected president. Congressman George Bush had been reelected without a struggle.

George W. was also in a good position. He was in the Texas Air National Guard, where he could fulfill his military duty without much danger. Also, he had been accepted for pilot training, even though he had no aviation experience. At the end of November he drove his blue Triumph convertible to Moody Air Force Base at Valdosta, Georgia, to report for a year of pilot training. He was made a second lieutenant, though he hadn't gone to officer candidate school.

Later in George W.'s life, critics would say that Congressman Bush had pulled strings to get his son these favors. But sons of influential men didn't necessarily have to *ask* for favors. Other people tended to give them favors without being asked. George's fellow pilot trainees in Georgia knew he had gotten special treatment, but they liked him anyway. George was a good pilot, and he had a talent for reading complicated mechanical charts and memorizing the entire structure of an airplane. Besides, as always he was cheerful, outgoing, and fun to be around.

Piloting a plane demands total concentration, fast reactions, and a quick, practical mind. George took to it happily. He trained on the F-102, which the pilots called a "sports car" because it could climb so quickly. He was very aware of the danger, but that was part of the excitement. "One mistake and you could end up in a very expensive metal coffin," he said.

The other pilots respected the way George W. handled a plane, but they were most impressed with him for his date with Tricia Nixon, the president's daughter. While the other trainees were stuck at the base, President Nixon sent a government plane all the way from Andrews Air Force Base, near Washington, D.C., to southern Georgia to pick George up. He was ferried to Washington, where he escorted Tricia out to dinner, and then he was ferried back.

Back at the base George's friends grilled him and teased him about his date, but he wouldn't talk. "It wasn't a very long date," was his only comment. He knew better than to gossip about Tricia Nixon. If you went out with the daughter of the president of the United States, it didn't matter if you had a good time, a bad time, or just a so–so time—you kept your mouth shut.

George W. might have been reckless about some things, but not his father's political career. Congressman Bush had already decided to run for the Senate next year. This was taking a risk, since Bush had to give up his safe seat in the House of Representatives to campaign for the Senate. But President Nixon was not only encouraging him, but campaigning for him and contributing money. The Bush family had high hopes.

CHAPTER 7
WHAT NEXT?

IN DECEMBER 1969 GEORGE W. BUSH RECEIVED HIS National Guard wings. He was moved from Georgia back to Houston. There he could live off base while he continued his pilot training and flew night maneuvers at Ellington Air Force Base.

In January 1970 George Bush announced his entry into the race for senator. He had the backing of powerful Republicans, including President Nixon. They wanted liberal Democratic senator Ralph Yarborough replaced with a Republican.

Although George W. wasn't free to campaign for his father that spring, his military service as a pilot was turned into good publicity for his father. In March an article about Second Lieutenant Bush appeared in the Houston papers. George W. had just completed his first solo flight in the

F-102 fighter plane. "George Walker Bush is one member of the younger generation who doesn't get his kicks from [drugs]," the article began. It went on to quote George W. explaining how he felt about flying a fighter plane by himself: "It was really neat. It was fun, and very exciting."

The article added, pointedly, that Lieutenant Bush was the son of U.S. representative George Bush, a former World War II navy fighter pilot who was running for the U.S. Senate. In promilitary Texas it helped to remind voters that patriotism and military service were important to both George H. W. Bush and his son.

Around the nation the disturbing and confusing times were not over. College students continued to protest the Vietnam War. In May, National Guardsmen in Ohio faced an unruly crowd of protesters at Kent State University. The guardsmen fired into the crowd, and four people were killed.

During that summer George W. moved into a one-bedroom apartment in the Chateaux Dijon, a large, new complex in Houston, full of young single people like George W. There was always something going on—games of volleyball, water polo in one of the six swimming pools, and all kinds of parties.

George and Barbara Bush were now traveling around

Texas, in the full swing of the Senate campaign. Sometimes George W. went on short trips with his parents. Dressed in his National Guard flight jacket, he stood next to his father on the platform. For the first time in a campaign he would step up to the microphone to say a few words.

Around the pool at the Chateaux Dijon or with his National Guard buddies, George W. was always ready for a good time. But when he campaigned for his father, he was serious and disciplined. The college-aged interns who volunteered for the Bush campaign thought George W. seemed mature. He was twenty-four, only a couple of years older than they were, but he didn't go out partying with them or even use slang in front of them.

That summer Congressman Bush's campaign was in trouble. The Republicans had planned on facing Senator Yarborough, a liberal Democrat. But instead the more conservative Lloyd Bentsen won the Democratic primary. George Bush and Lloyd Bentsen had similar ideas about many of the issues, and it was tough for voters to distinguish between the two candidates' platforms.

In 1970 many Southern voters still preferred to vote Democratic. Lloyd Bentsen was a Democrat who had been raised in Texas, while George Bush had grown up in New England. Some Texans still considered Bush a Yankee. To Bush's dismay, Lloyd Bentsen won the election in November.

George Bush was crushed. He felt rejected by the Texas he loved. He had wanted very badly to serve in the Senate, and his friends and family had wanted very badly to see him there. Barbara and Doro sobbed openly. The men on the campaign, including George W., went off to cry behind closed doors.

Now George Bush wasn't even a congressman, because he'd had to give up that seat to run for senator. Early in 1971, however, President Nixon appointed him U.S. ambassador to the United Nations. George and Barbara moved to New York, the headquarters of the UN. Then they left for Europe to begin traveling on Ambassador Bush's new job.

Back in Houston, George W. wasn't sure what to do with himself. His admired father had been defeated again—most unfairly, it seemed. George W. had applied to the University of Texas law school in Austin, but he had been rejected. If he was going to follow in his father's footsteps, he'd have to go into the oil business at that point. But the last several years had been bad for the oil business in

Texas, as cheap oil flowed freely from the Arab countries.

George W. stayed in Houston, served his National Guard time on weekends—and partied. In early 1971 he took a job as a trainee for an agribusiness company. But the nine-to-five office work bored him. "A stupid coat-and-tie job," he called it. He quit after less than a year.

George W. was now wondering if he should go into politics. A seat in the Texas state senate was opening up, and he thought he might run for it in 1972. But his father had a better idea. His old friend and political advisor Jimmy Allison was working on Red Blount's campaign for the U.S. Senate in Alabama. George Bush thought it would be good experience for George W. to join that campaign.

Winton "Red" Blount, former U.S. postmaster general, was a conservative Republican and dedicated supporter of Richard Nixon. George W. moved to Alabama and worked as political director of his campaign through the summer and fall of 1972. A girlfriend who also joined the campaign was impressed with how hard George W. worked. "He put bumper stickers on in the parking lot, and believe me, that is the pits," she said. "At that time in Alabama, people would spit on you if you were a Republican."

But the campaign was a losing cause. Democratic senator

John Sparkman, running for reelection, was popular and personable. George W. noticed that his candidate, Red Blount, was not. President Nixon, also running for reelection, was doing well, but he did not come to Alabama to support Blount.

During the summer of 1972 there had been rumors that burglars working for President Nixon had broken into the Democratic Party's campaign headquarters in the Watergate Complex. But the White House denied the rumors, and they didn't damage the president's campaign. The Democratic candidate, Senator George McGovern, was nominated mainly because he was against the war in Vietnam. As election day neared, though, it seemed that the war would soon be over anyway. Richard Nixon was reelected by a landslide—only one state, Massachusetts, went for McGovern.

But for the Bushes, the election results were overshadowed by a family tragedy. Early in October, George W.'s grandfather Prescott Bush died of lung cancer. The Bush-Walker clan gathered in Greenwich, Connecticut, for the funeral. George W. and his brothers were pallbearers. Prescott Bush was buried in the cemetery next to the white marble marker for George's sister Robin.

During that winter George W. applied to Harvard Business School. A friend from Yale who had gone to Harvard Business School urged him to apply, but George W. wasn't sure about it. In January 1973 he went to work for the Professional United Leadership League (PULL), an inner-city youth program in Houston.

The idea of PULL was to give mentors to minority kids in the inner city. Professional basketball, baseball, or football players, who could use their off-season to work with the boys, could be ideal role models. The program had been started by a former pro football player, John L. White. George W.'s father was honorary chairman.

George W. took naturally to this job. He was good at fund-raising, and he had many connections with wealthy people. He loved working with kids, and he loved being around professional athletes. Also, he felt for these boys, growing up in neighborhoods where life was a constant struggle against crime and poverty. He was eager to make a difference in their lives.

George W. especially took to one six-year-old boy, Jimmy Dean. If Jimmy showed up at the center without shoes, George took him out and bought shoes for him. Jimmy would hang on George's leg, as if they had adopted each other.

All the boys in PULL loved George W. He played basketball and Ping-Pong with them; he took them to prisons to show them the results of breaking the law. Once, he even took them for an airplane ride, the first time any of them had ever been in an airplane. Up in the air, one of the boys started kidding around, making a lot of noise. George W. stalled the engine for a moment—and there wasn't another peep out of the passengers.

Meanwhile, at the end of 1972 George W.'s father had begun a new job for President Nixon. He was now the chairman of the Republican National Committee, and the elder Bushes were living in Washington again. Doro and Neil were living with their parents and going to school in Washington. Jeb was at the University of Texas, and Marvin was at boarding school in Virginia.

Barbara Bush had pleaded with her husband not to accept the RNC chairmanship. The Republican Party was going through upheaval, in spite of President Nixon's triumphant reelection. Of course, no one knew how bad things were about to get, for Richard Nixon or for the Republican Party.

But George W. had his suspicions about Nixon and his staff. At the Republican National Convention the previous

64

summer, he'd taken time to chat with a friend from Yale who was working for the Nixon campaign. George W. asked his friend about the Watergate break-in story. "If there isn't something going on," George W. told him, "it sure looks like it, because nobody acts innocent."

CHAPTER 8

HOME FROM EXILE

"I HAD DABBLED IN MANY THINGS," GEORGE W. Bush said later, "but I had no real idea what I wanted to do with the rest of my life when I arrived at Harvard Business School." He hadn't even been sure he should leave PULL, where he knew he was doing good work, to go to business school. But John White, his boss at PULL, had urged him to try it. If George made a lot of money and gained power, White pointed out, he could do even more good for inner-city children. George's parents also thought that business school was a good idea—they hoped it would make him more self-disciplined.

In the fall of 1973, when George W. arrived, the Harvard campus was seething with student protests against government and business. George felt even more out of place than he had at Yale five years ago. His father—and practically everyone in the Bush-Walker family—believed deeply in government and business. George was not about to be disloyal to them.

However, that didn't mean that George was always mature and respectful. Just last Christmas, while he was visiting his parents in Washington, he'd had too much to drink at a party. On his way home he hit a neighbor's garbage can, and he drove into his parents' driveway with the can clanging under his car. Then, when his father got angry, he'd tried to pick a fight with him. But George W. would never take a stand against his father's deepest values.

The Harvard Business School itself was fairly conservative compared to the rest of the university. But George W. was more openly defiant of Harvard values than most of his classmates. He didn't hesitate to walk around campus in his well-worn Texas Air National Guard flight jacket. George W. was proud of his stint in the guard and proud of his training as a fighter pilot.

In Washington speculation about President Nixon's involvement in the Watergate break-in continued to grow. Even before George W. arrived at Harvard, news had come out that Nixon had taped conversations in the Oval Office of the White House. By November of 1973 even the Harvard Republican Club had voted to ask President Nixon to resign.

George W. lived quietly at Harvard. He made some good friends in the business school, but he stuck to a disciplined schedule of studying, running, riding his bike, and attending classes. When friends came to Boston to visit, he would take them to the Hillbilly Ranch, a country-and-western joint. Here, his friends noticed, George seemed comfortable, talking about Texas and chewing tobacco.

Weekends, George often went to visit his aunt Nancy Bush Ellis in Boston. Her home was a refuge from the Harvard campus, where it was normal to sneer at President Nixon and anyone who supported him. That "anyone," of course, included George W.'s father.

George H. W. Bush had been a Nixon supporter since 1952, when Richard Nixon was Dwight D. Eisenhower's running mate. By the summer of 1974, however, Bush had become convinced that the president had lied about Watergate. At that point he wrote President Nixon a letter, urging him to resign.

At the beginning of August, President Richard Nixon did resign. On August 9 the Nixons walked out of the White House for the last time, toward the helicopter pad.

Republican National Committee chairman George Bush and his wife, Barbara, loyally stood on the South Lawn of the White House as the Nixons waved and climbed into the waiting helicopter.

Gerald Ford, Richard Nixon's vice president, was now president. He considered choosing George Bush for his vice president, but in the end he chose Nelson Rockefeller instead. To Bush he gave the job of acting as unofficial ambassador to China. The United States did not yet have full diplomatic relations with China, but clearly this country would be important in the future.

In the spring of 1975 George W. graduated from Harvard Business School. That March he visited a friend in the Southwest, and he stopped in Midland to see his mentor Jimmy Allison. Allison told him that West Texas was in the middle of a second oil boom, and George could see for himself that it was true. Newcomers were pouring into Midland. The price of oil had soared from two dollars a barrel to thirty-six dollars a barrel.

Finally George W. knew what he wanted to do next. In the Middle East the oil-producing countries had decided to export less oil so that prices would rise. The United States had become so dependent on cheap oil from the

Middle East that there was now an oil shortage in the country. And once again there were great opportunities in Midland, where the elder George Bush had made his fortune in the 1950s.

With a light heart, George W. made plans to leave the Northeast. He was grateful for his business school education, but he was delighted to leave Cambridge.

"Claustrophobic," he called the feeling Harvard gave him. It was a physical feeling of being closed in, breathing stuffy air, living walled off from the rest of the country. In his Harvard Business School yearbook picture George W. looks as if he were already in West Texas. His face is tanned, and instead of the usual suit and tie, he's wearing a wrinkled polo shirt, open at the neck.

In the summer of 1975 George W., Neil, and Marvin went to China to visit George, Barbara, and Doro in Beijing. Jeb Bush, who had just gotten married, stayed in Houston. On the Fourth of July the Bushes invited five hundred Chinese guests to an American-style cookout. (There was an emergency the week before—it was nearly impossible to get seven hundred hot dog rolls in Communist China!) The Bush children, including George W., all helped hand out hot dogs and hamburgers.

Touring around China, George was struck with how drab and monotonous the people's clothes were. Bicycles, too, all looked exactly the same. He was thankful to return to the United States, where the free market let individuals choose what to sell and what to buy.

Back in Texas in the fall of 1975, George W. moved to Midland. Immediately he felt at home again. "The sky's the limit" was the Midland city motto. That sense of unlimited possibilities suited George W. perfectly.

Many of his parents' friends from the 1950s, such as Jimmy Allison, were still there. Some of his own childhood friends had moved away and then come back, just as George had.

One of these friends was Joe O'Neill, who had tried so hard to imitate Mr. Bush's trick of catching fly balls behind his back. Joe was now married and working in his family's oil business.

Another old friend was Randy Roden, the boy next door when the Bushes were living on Easter Egg Row. Charlie Younger was a few years older than George, but they knew each other from the Ohio Street neighborhood. Charlie ran every day, like George, and he also liked to joke as much as George did. And then there was Susie Evans, now married to Don Evans, who also worked in the oil business.

George W. rented an apartment and settled into his usual free-form style of housekeeping. The floor was strewn with newspapers and magazines and heaps of laundry. The broken bed frame was held together with a necktie.

Midland welcomed George W., with his nonstop energy and his passion for having fun. He started every day by running around the high school stadium. On Sundays he went to the First Presbyterian Church and taught Sunday school. He played golf and went to the Midland Angels games.

George and his friends who ran around the track together gave one another nicknames. He was "the Bombastic Bushkin." After George W.'s two years in Cambridge, Massachusetts, Midland felt blissfully comfortable to him.

In Midland there was no need for a suit or a tie (except to hold his bed together). He could wear cowboy boots. In fact, when he was trying to talk a rancher into leasing the oil rights to his land, it was better *not* to look like a smarty-pants Ivy League graduate. If George did have to dress up once in a while, he'd wear one of the cheap suits he'd picked up in China. They didn't fit that well, and his friends always teased him.

They also teased him about his Chinese slippers. One night he was wearing them when some friends came over for dinner. They teased him until George issued a challenge: "I bet I could beat you running the track—even in these slippers." His friends thought that was a great joke, but they all trotted over to the high school track. George did beat them, although he ran his slippers to shreds in the process.

George was famous among his friends for not wanting to spend money. For a joke, one of his buddies bought a shabby used sweater in a thrift shop and presented it to George. George wasn't embarrassed at all—in fact, he wore that sweater for a long time.

To get started in the oil business, George W. went to an old friend of his parents', Walter Holton. Walter advised George to work as a "landman." A landman went to the county courthouse and looked up deeds to find out who owned the oil rights on a piece of land. Then he might arrange for a company drilling for oil to lease the land. More important, a landman could work for himself, which suited George.

George W. began to invest some of his own money in small oil wells. He hoped to make his fortune in business, as his father had. But he also had another reason: He was starting to get serious about going into politics, and he didn't want to have to depend on someone else's money.

CHAPTER 9
GETTING SERIOUS

IN JULY 1976, AFTER ALMOST A YEAR BACK IN
midland, George W. Bush turned thirty years old. His
business was going fairly well, and he decided to call it
Bush Oil. He moved into a tiny office—actually, it was the
watercooler room in a friend's office. Visitors had to sit on
Coke crates.

Nineteen seventy-six was a landmark year for the
country, too: The United States was two hundred years old.
It was also a presidential election year. Democrat Jimmy
Carter, governor of Georgia, was running against Repub-
lican president Gerald Ford. George W. Bush worked for
President Ford's campaign in West Texas.

George W.'s parents were back from China and living
in Washington, D.C., again. At the end of 1975 President
Ford had asked George Bush to become director of the

Central Intelligence Agency, or CIA. Bush wasn't sure that he wanted the job, and he called George W. to get his opinion.

"Take the job and come home," said George W. "We want you home." As it turned out, that job would last only a year. Jimmy Carter won the White House in November 1976 and then CIA director George Bush was out of a job.

Meanwhile, George W. began to make small investments in oil wells. The first try was a big shock to him. The oil well was drilled, it turned out to be dry, and just like that, George lost the few thousand dollars he had invested. For a man who hated to spend money even for a new sweater, or a new bed frame, that hurt. But the experience taught George W. a lot about the ups and downs of the business, and luckily the next few holes produced some oil.

Ever since he'd moved to Midland, George W. had been looking for a chance to run for Congress. In 1977 he consulted his father about his new plans. The seat for the Nineteenth Congressional District in West Texas would probably be open next year, and George W. was thinking of running for U.S. representative.

George H. W. Bush was "tickled pink," he wrote to a

friend, that his first son was following the family tradition into politics. The rest of George W.'s family and friends enthusiastically stepped up to support him. His friends with wealthy connections, including Joe O'Neill and Don Evans, promised that money would be no problem.

The national Republican Party was very interested in helping a Republican win the seat in the Nineteenth District. Texas was an important state, and winning this race might make a big difference. Karl Rove, a sharp, young political advisor who had worked for the elder Bush, came to Midland to help George W. His brother, Neil Bush, who had just graduated from college, moved to Texas to comanage George W.'s campaign.

In August 1977 George W. had just begun his campaign when Joe O'Neill and his wife, Jan, invited him over to meet someone. They wanted to introduce him to Laura Welch, a former roommate of Jan's. Laura was a librarian at an elementary school in Austin, but she had grown up in Midland. In fact, both Laura and George had gone to San Jacinto Junior High, although they hadn't really known each other then. By coincidence, in the early 1970s both of them had lived at the Chateaux Dijon apartments in Houston. But Laura lived on the quiet side of the complex, while George had been on the rowdy side, and they had never met.

Laura wasn't at all sure she wanted to meet George W. Bush. She knew he came from a very political family, and she had no interest in politics. But at the O'Neills' that evening in August she was surprised at what a good time she was having. She relaxed and found herself laughing. She definitely liked the Bombastic Bushkin.

As for George, he was immediately taken with Laura. She was beautiful. And as he talked and talked with his usual nonstop energy, he became aware that this quiet, poised, intelligent woman was not just laughing at his jokes. She was really paying attention to him. The next night he invited her out for miniature golf.

Shortly afterward George W. joined his family in Kennebunkport, Maine. He told them right away that he had met someone. Of course, George was always meeting women. But his family knew this was different. He hadn't been this serious about anyone since he was in college, engaged to Cathryn Wolfman. He even cut short his vacation in Maine to return to Texas—and Laura.

Many people who knew both of them were amazed that boisterous George W. Bush and ladylike librarian Laura

Welch were interested in each other. Even the O'Neills, who had introduced Laura and George, were surprised that they hit it off so well. As a Texas journalist remarked, "Bush was exactly the kind of guy librarians would tell to shut up in the library."

In October, George W. took Laura to Houston to meet his family. His brother Jeb wasn't about to pass up this chance to tease George. Greeting them at the front door, he dropped to one knee like an old-fashioned suitor. "Did you pop the question to her, George, old boy?"

George blushed and, for once, couldn't think of anything to say. But Laura spoke up. "Yes, as a matter of fact he has, and I accepted."

George W. and Laura didn't want a big, fancy wedding, and they didn't want to wait too long. Since George W.'s parents had a very busy schedule, they picked a date in November when George and Barbara Bush could be there. They were married in Midland at the First United Methodist Church, where Laura's family belonged.

Right after the wedding George W. hit the campaign trail. He was sure they could manage their new marriage and a run for office at the same time. Of course he understood that Laura didn't like politics, although he would need her support in the campaign. But he promised that she wouldn't have to make any speeches without him.

A few months later George W. took the promise back. He was scheduled to speak in a town called Muleshoe, but something else came up. Laura would have to fill in for him. So Laura found herself on the courthouse steps in Muleshoe, giving her first campaign speech. Nervous and trembling, she lost track of what she was saying. It was like a nightmare.

Later in the campaign Laura forgot an important piece of advice from her new mother-in-law, Barbara Bush. Barbara had lived through two campaigns for the U.S. Senate and two campaigns for the House of Representatives with George W.'s father, and they were still happily married. "Don't criticize his speeches," she'd told Laura.

But this advice slipped Laura's mind, one night when they were driving home from a campaign appearance. All the way home George W. kept asking what she thought of his speech. "Tell me the truth," he urged one last time as he turned into their driveway. "I didn't do very well, did I?"

"No, it wasn't very good," she answered.

Stunned, George W. drove the car right into the garage wall. He knew politics was a rough game, and he could take criticism from a lot of people: his political rivals, newspaper reporters, his advisors. But it was difficult to take criticism from his wife—even if she was right!

In June 1978 George W. Bush won the primary race. It was an impressive victory, because some influential Republicans, including Ronald Reagan, were supporting his opponent. But in November he lost the election to his Democratic opponent.

The Democrats had managed to portray George W. as an Eastern carpetbagger, a Yale and Harvard boy with no real roots in Texas. George W. was furious. He loved Texas more than any place in the world. He had grown up in Texas and lived there most of his life.

Losing was a bad disappointment, but George W. was not giving up on politics. He'd been through it with his father. The elder George Bush had lost his first campaign, but he'd won the second.

For now George W. would get on with his oil business. He was launching his own drilling company, Arbusto Energy. *Arbusto* is Spanish for "bush" or "shrub." George's uncle Jonathan, who owned a New York investment firm, helped raise the money to get Arbusto started.

At the same time, in the spring of 1979, there was a

new Bush political campaign to think about. George W.'s father had decided to run for president in 1980. The whole Bush family joined the campaign. Even George W., in the middle of launching Arbusto, made trips for his father. The primary elections were a year away, but there would be a fierce fight for the Republican nomination.

Ronald Reagan, Republican governor of California, had also decided to go for the presidency. By May of 1980 Ronald Reagan had won enough primaries to capture the Republican Party's nomination. Bush had to admit defeat, and he sent a telegram of gracious congratulations to Reagan.

To a friend in the CIA, George H. W. Bush wrote of his private feelings, "No one died but it feels like it." George W., too, was deeply disappointed that his father wouldn't get a chance to win in November. If any man deserved to be president, he believed, it was George Herbert Walker Bush.

On the other hand, George W. had to admire Ronald Reagan's style. At a time when voters were fed up with big government and Washington politicians, Reagan presented himself as a relaxed, easygoing Westerner. He made people feel good about themselves, about America—and about Ronald Reagan. Also, Reagan had a very clear political message: He was conservative, and he was proud of it.

At the Republican National Convention in Detroit, Ronald Reagan asked George Bush to run with him, for vice president. George W. had thought this might happen, and he was glad when his father accepted. In November the Republican ticket won a sweeping victory over Democratic president Jimmy Carter.

CHAPTER 10
THE VICE PRESIDENT'S SON

IN JANUARY 1981 GEORGE W. AND LAURA BUSH went to Washington for the presidential inauguration. George W., standing near his father on the west side of the Capitol, watched proudly as George Herbert Walker Bush took the oath of office as vice president of the United States. George W. had wanted his father to be president, of course, but he also realized that the 1980 race had not been his father's time. It was Ronald Reagan's time. In politics, timing was everything.

Only two months later it seemed that George H. W. Bush might soon become president, after all. George W. was in the Arbusto office in Midland when shocking news came over the radio. President Reagan had been shot and seriously wounded by an assassin.

George told his secretary to keep the phone lines free,

in case his father called. He was deeply shaken, thinking of what this meant to the country and to his father. If the president died, the vice president would immediately be sworn in as president. George W. knew Vice President Bush had been on his way to Austin, but now he would fly back to Washington for the emergency. As it turned out, President Reagan recovered quickly.

That summer, George W. had something very personal to be happy about. He and Laura were expecting a baby before the end of 1981. They both loved children, and they were eager for a family of their own. So it was double good news when they learned Laura was carrying twins.

But it wasn't an easy pregnancy. Laura suffered from toxemia, a condition that causes high blood pressure, headaches, and swelling. Laura's doctor, worried about her health, delivered the twins in November, a month early. George W. was relieved and overjoyed. His wife was safe, and now he had *two* daughters. They named the girls Jenna Welch Bush, for Laura's mother, and Barbara Pierce Bush, for George's mother.

In January, George W.'s parents visited the new family of four in Midland. They were touched and amused to see their first son—little Georgie!—now juggling two tiny babies of his own. At first the twins seemed to cry all the time. "What's the matter with them?" the worried father would ask Laura. But she didn't know either.

Sometimes George W. would take both squalling babies and walk back and forth, jiggling them and making faces to try to stop their crying. He'd sing them the Yale fight song: "Bulldog, bulldog. Bowwow-wow." The best times for the new parents were quiet early mornings, feeding the babies. Laura and George W. would each take a baby and a bottle and settle cozily back into bed with their coffee and newspapers.

As the girls grew George had a great time with them. He changed diapers, fed them, took them for walks in the stroller. He wiggled his ears at them to make them laugh. When they were a little older, he would get down on the floor and tickle them and wrestle with them.

Meanwhile, George W.'s business, Arbusto Energy, wasn't doing particularly well. Unlike his father, George W. wasn't lucky at striking oil. When the oil business was booming, he did all right. But in 1982 a slump in the oil business began. Soon George W. was struggling just to keep his company afloat.

• • •

In 1984 President Reagan and Vice President Bush were up for reelection. President Reagan was very popular, and there wasn't much doubt that they would win. George W. went to the Republican National Convention in Dallas that August. There was no suspense, of course, about who the nominees would be. George W. was more interested in what people were thinking about possible candidates for 1988, four years from then. To him, the choice would be obvious: Vice President George H. W. Bush.

After the Republican convention George W. flew to Tennessee to help with a friend's campaign. Victor Ashe, whom George knew from Yale, was running for senator against Democrat Al Gore Jr. George W. knew that Ashe didn't have much of a chance running against popular Congressman Gore in a Democratic state. But he was a loyal friend, and the campaign was good political experience for him.

On election day in November, President Reagan won over Democratic candidate Walter Mondale by the expected landslide. Vice President Bush would be back in Washington for another four years at least. In 1985 the Bush family began planning for the election of 1988.

Meanwhile, "Bombastic" George W. was becoming

more thoughtful and mature. At the Methodist church in Midland he attended Bible study classes. He studied lessons from the Bible in the same intense way he'd once memorized baseball statistics or the parts of a fighter plane.

The Reverend Billy Graham, a famous evangelist preacher, had been a friend of the Bush family ever since George W. was young. Now George had serious discussions with the reverend about personal spiritual questions. Friends and family began to see a change in George—he wasn't so quick to lose his temper.

More and more, George realized how precious Laura and his daughters were to him. Jenna and Barbara constantly delighted him. He loved to lie on the floor and read them Dr. Seuss's *Hop on Pop*—and let the girls actually hop on him. He loved to watch the twins "teach" their dolls, lining them up in rows and drilling them on their lessons. "We have the best-educated dolls in America," George joked to Laura.

By the end of 1985 the oil industry in Texas was suffering. Oil prices had collapsed. George W.'s own business was in very bad shape—in fact, it was in danger of going bankrupt. To avoid an imminent shutdown, he sold out to Harken Energy in the spring of 1986.

George W. Bush was now almost forty. So was Laura, and so were their good friends Joe and Jan O'Neill and Don and Susie Evans. In June 1986 the whole group of friends went to the luxurious Broadmoor Hotel in Colorado Springs to celebrate. After a night of drinking, George W. woke up with a fierce headache.

He managed to go for his usual morning run in spite of the pain, but that day he realized Laura was right. She had been telling him for some time that he needed to stop drinking. When he drank too much alcohol, it was easy for him to lose his temper. And it was easy for him to make smart remarks that weren't as funny as he thought.

Back at the hotel from his run, George W. told Laura, "I'm quitting drinking." He also told Joe O'Neill, but no one else. From that day on, George just didn't drink anymore.

"I felt different," he said. "I had more time to read. I had more energy. I became a better listener, and not such an incessant talker. Quitting drinking made me more focused and more disciplined."

There were several reasons that George W. was now determined to be the best that he could be. One of them, of course, was his children. Another was his father's campaign for president in 1988. George W. was eager to throw himself into the campaign with everything he had.

Also, from all his experience in politics George W. was keenly aware that the media would now spotlight every part of his father's life. As the son of a presidential candidate George W. couldn't afford to drink too much and say or do foolish things. It might hurt his father's chances to win.

As Vice President Bush's campaign got under way in 1986, George W. wanted to make sure that each person on the Bush team was absolutely loyal to his father. Meeting his father's campaign strategist, Lee Atwater, he had one all-important question: "How do we know we can trust you?"

"What he means," added George's brother Jeb, "is, if someone throws a grenade at our dad, we expect you to jump on it."

The Bushes weren't expecting real grenades; Jeb was using an expression from military combat. If the enemy lobbed a grenade at an officer, a good soldier would fling himself on top of it. He would sacrifice his life to shield his officer from the explosion. That was the kind of loyalty George W. wanted to see in every last person working for his father.

Lee Atwater agreed, and he thought George W. was

just the one to make sure everyone on the Bush team was loyal. "Why don't you come to Washington and help me with the campaign?" he asked. In April 1987 George W. and his family did move to Washington, and he began working full-time on getting his father elected. Traveling around the country, he campaigned hard for his father, often speaking in his place. The campaign workers regarded him and his mother as the best stand-ins for the candidate.

During this campaign George W. got to be good friends with Lee Atwater, one of the few people he allowed to call him "Junior." He agreed with Atwater that his father needed to work on his image. Too many people saw him as an Eastern aristocrat, out of touch with the lives of ordinary people.

No one was angrier than George W. when an October 1987 issue of *Newsweek* came out. The cover showed Vice President Bush at the family retreat in Kennebunkport, steering his cigarette boat. The Bush team knew the article was coming, but they had no idea it would be so hard on the vice president. The headline was FIGHTING THE WIMP FACTOR. The idea of the article was that voters didn't see George Bush as brave enough or tough enough to be president.

The vice president wrote in his diary, "That *Newsweek* story was the cheapest shot I've seen in my political life." George W. raged, "They were talking about George Bush, war hero, youngest pilot to earn his wings in the Navy, a pilot who had been shot down . . . near an island occupied by the Japanese. . . . I let a lot of people know exactly how I felt."

At the Republican National Convention in New Orleans in the summer of 1988, George W. was the spokesperson for the Texas delegation. He had the pleasure of announcing the votes that put his father over the top as the Republican nominee. "One hundred and eleven votes for Texas's favorite son and the world's best father!"

At the Democratic National Convention, Ann Richards of Texas was the keynote speaker. Part of her job, of course, was to charge up the assembled Democrats and tear down the Republican opposition. Ann Richards had a sharp tongue, and she made a witty remark about Vice President Bush that was picked up by all the media: "Poor George, he can't help it . . . he was born with a silver foot in his mouth." Barbara Bush, watching the convention on TV from Kennebunkport, was sickened. She never forgave Ann Richards for that remark—and neither did George W.

For the most part, the year and a half of the campaign was a happy time for George W. He loved living in Washington, near his parents. He and Laura and their girls would go over to the vice president's residence for Sunday cookouts. When George and Laura went out of town, the twins could stay with their grandparents.

One of these overnights took place the day before Vice President Bush was scheduled for a televised debate with his opponent, Michael Dukakis. Little Barbara couldn't get to sleep that night, because she'd lost her special stuffed dog, Spikey. So instead of getting rested up for the debate, "Gampy" Bush spent hours searching the house and grounds with a flashlight. He finally found Spikey.

But the debate must have gone all right, in spite of Spikey. On election day in November 1988, Vice President George Bush won a firm victory over Massachusetts governor Michael Dukakis.

CHAPTER 11

THE PRESIDENT'S SON

EARLY ON THE MORNING AFTER ELECTION DAY, 1988, the Bushes held a private service at St. Martin's Episcopal Church in Houston. George W. said a special prayer of thanksgiving. His parents were deeply touched to hear him ask for guidance. "Particularly watch over Dad and Mother," he prayed. "Dad" was now the president-elect of the United States.

Then George and Barbara Bush flew back to Washington, along with George W., Laura, and the twins. The girls, almost seven, were wild with excitement. They crammed wads of paper into the plane's toilet and stopped it up. Their grandmother, even though she was almost First Lady, was the one to pull the paper out.

• • •

At the end of 1988 George W. moved his family to Dallas. He was still an unofficial advisor to his father, but he had decided to take on a new project in Texas. He would gather a group of investors to buy the Texas Rangers baseball team. George W. himself would invest only a small amount, but he would be the public spokesman for the group. Being in the spotlight, getting people to give money, getting people to work together—these were exactly the things George W. was good at.

In May the new First Lady came to Dallas to visit. Barbara Bush brought a springer spaniel puppy, one of her dog Millie's litter, for her granddaughters. But the puppy, Spot, soon decided she was George W.'s dog, and George and Spot spent a lot of time playing ball.

George W. had invited his mother to throw out the first pitch at a Rangers game. He thought it would be good publicity for the Rangers and for himself, but also for his mother. Barbara Bush was promoting a national literacy program, Reading Is Fundamental, and he publicized the program at the game.

At the baseball park Barbara noticed that her son was in his glory as the spokesman for the Texas Rangers owners. He loved hanging out with professional baseball players, athletes like the ones he had idolized as a boy. And he seemed to know the name of every single person in the ball park, including the ticket takers and hot dog vendors.

This job was a great way for George W. Bush to get his name known in Texas before he ran for office again. At every game he was in his box seat near the Rangers' dugout, in full view of the cameras. He had baseball cards printed with his own picture on them, and he signed them and handed them out to fans.

George W. had been thinking of running for governor of Texas in 1990, but he decided it was too soon. Voters still knew him mainly as the son of a famous father. As long as the elder George Bush was president, it would be difficult for George W. not to be overshadowed. So in 1990 Republican Clayton Williams, an oil millionaire from Midland, ran against Democrat Ann Richards for governor. Ann Richards won.

In 1991 the Bush clan and their allies began working to reelect President Bush in 1992. But for the president himself the first months of the year were consumed with the war in Iraq, Operation Desert Storm. Iraq, led by Saddam Hussein, had invaded Kuwait, threatening American oil supplies. The U.S. responded by bombing Iraq, following up with an attack on the ground. The war was over in just a few days.

Most Americans admired President Bush for his conduct of the war. In the polls his popularity was at a high of 89 percent. But in other ways bad publicity plagued the Bushes. George W. was investigated by the Securities and Exchange Commission. He was accused of deliberately selling his stock in Harken, the company that had bought Arbusto. His critics charged that he had deliberately sold stock at a time he knew the stock was about to go down.

The year before, George W.'s brother Neil had been blamed for playing a role in the failure of Denver's Silverado Savings and Loan. Neil served as a board member of Silverado, but George was sure his brother had nothing to do with its collapse. "He's probably got the biggest heart in the family," he said, "and there's not a devious bone in his body."

Now President Bush was having problems with his staff. John Sununu, the White House chief of staff, was pompous and arrogant, and he offended many people. He was criticized in the media for using government jets and limousines for personal travel. Worse, Sununu seemed to be more ambitious for his own career than loyal to the president. He said things to the press that made the president look bad. In November, speaking on TV, Sununu said President Bush had "ad-libbed" a recent remark that caused the stock market to fall. Whether Sununu meant it or not, he made it sound as if the president couldn't be trusted to make his own remarks.

George W. was furious. John Sununu had violated the Bushes' chief value: loyalty. "We have a saying in our family," he told reporters. "If the grenade is rolling by The Man, you dive on it first."

Flying to Washington, George W. spoke privately to Sununu. "It might be in everybody's interest if you would step aside," he said bluntly. At the beginning of December, John Sununu resigned his position as chief of staff.

By the spring of 1992 George W. was even more concerned about his father's chances for reelection. Another Republican candidate, Pat Robertson of the Christian Right, did alarmingly well in the New Hampshire Republican primary. In Texas, President Bush's home state, many voters were enthusiastic about Reform Party candidate Ross Perot.

But meanwhile, the Bushes were enjoying their time in the White House. In May, Queen Elizabeth II of England came to visit. George W. and Laura were included in a lunch during the queen's stay. Jokingly, the First Lady told Her Majesty that she'd seated her oldest son at the other end of the table because he was sure to say or do the wrong thing. In fact, he'd threatened to wear cowboy boots to the formal state dinner that evening. The queen thought this was very funny. That night, when George W. came through the receiving line, she glanced pointedly at his feet. He grinned and pulled up his trouser legs enough to show his cowboy boots—with American flags on them.

Unfortunately, many voters felt that President George H. W. Bush was too much like English royalty. (He was actually a distant relative of Queen Elizabeth II.) His rivals called him "out of touch" with the average American family, and they were quick to remind people of his upbringing in New England private schools. Also, he had a gentlemanly manner—he didn't seem like a regular guy.

By June 1992 public opinion polls showed that President Bush was running behind Democratic candidate Bill Clinton *and* Reform Party candidate Ross Perot. Many Republicans urged President Bush to dump Vice President Dan Quayle and pick someone who would attract more voters. George W. began working full-time on his father's campaign. That August both President Bush and his son had to skip the Bush-Walker family gathering in Kennebunkport.

At the Republican National Convention in Houston, George W. accused journalists of having a bias against President Bush. George W. and other members of the Bush-Walker clan worked hard to arouse enthusiasm for George Bush's reelection. But it seemed that President Bush had started to campaign too late, and his message to the people wasn't focused enough. During September and October, it became increasingly clear that the Democratic nominee, Bill Clinton, would win the White House in November. The economy was dragging, and people blamed President Bush for that.

George W. was hurt for his father, fearing that he would soon be a one-term president, like Jimmy Carter. He felt that Bill Clinton and Al Gore's campaign against his father was unfair, and he hated to watch it. He compared it to mud wrestling. "It's hard to be a joyful participant in a mud-wrestling contest," he told a reporter, "when someone you really care about is getting mud wrestled."

To the very end, President George Bush believed that he would be reelected. But the day before the election, as

George W. and his father sat together on *Air Force One*, the Oak Ridge Boys sang a mournful song that pointed to the outcome of this presidential race. "Almost all of us had tears in our eyes when they sang 'Amazing Grace,'" the president noted in his diary. George W. told his father, "You've run a great campaign—there's nothing more you can do."

Late on the afternoon of election day, George W. called up his parents and gave them the bad news from the exit polls. They were going to lose this one.

CHAPTER 12

GOVERNOR GEORGE W. BUSH

EVEN DURING THE HEAT OF HIS FATHER'S CAMPAIGN for reelection, George W. Bush had been thinking about running for governor of Texas in 1994. He mentioned it to his friend Charlie Younger in June 1992 when they were in Kennebunkport with their wives. "You're crazy," was Charlie's response.

With a governor like Ann Richards, why would Texans want to elect anyone else? Texas seemed to love Governor Richards, the smart-talking, silver-haired, motorcycle-riding grandmother. She was a real Texan, from a poor background, but she was also a national celebrity.

But other advisors gave George W. different advice. Alphonso Jackson, an African-American Republican leader in Texas, said, "The best time to run against somebody is when they're at their best." He meant that Governor Ann

Richards was riding high—she and her supporters would be overconfident. Also, while Texans loved Ann Richards, that didn't mean they loved her policies. Many voters thought she was too liberal. For instance, they didn't like her idea of raising money for poorer school districts by taxing wealthy districts.

Toward the end of 1992, while he was thinking about the coming race for governor, George W. began training to run the Houston Marathon. Every day he jogged several miles. In January he and Laura went to stay with his parents in Houston during the marathon. They cheered him on while he ran the twenty-six mile race in three hours and forty-four minutes.

So George W. had proved he had the stamina to run a marathon. He knew he had the stamina to run for governor, too. During the spring he gathered a team to plan his strategy. The Bush team included old family friends who could raise large amounts of money and people who were important in the Republican Party. It also included the brilliant political strategist Karl Rove.

One person who *wasn't* enthusiastic about George running for governor was Laura Bush. She wondered if he wanted to run for the right reasons. Maybe this was his way of carrying on the Bush political dynasty, inherited from his father and his grandfather, Senator Prescott Bush. And although she didn't say, "You're crazy," she wondered if George W. really stood a chance against popular, famous Governor Ann Richards.

Karl Rove insisted that Richards's popularity wasn't that deep. "They like her hair," he said, "but they're not that strongly anchored to her." There were rumors that Lieutenant Governor Bob Bullock, a powerful political figure in Texas, was dissatisfied with Richards. He thought she was *too* popular, enjoying her celebrity too much.

That summer, 1993, Bush people began leaking hints that George W. might run. The idea was to build up publicity before his official announcement. Then, after the end of baseball season that fall, George W. Bush publicly announced that he was running for governor of Texas. Unfortunately, the *Houston Chronicle* published the wrong picture to go with the announcement. It was a picture of the *other* George Bush, his father.

The last thing George W. wanted was to be overshadowed by his famous father. But he didn't let this little mishap discourage him. He hit the road, speaking in twenty-seven cities in five days. George W. had learned one very important thing from watching his father's defeat the year before. *He* was starting his campaign early, and he was campaigning hard from the start.

Another thing George W. had learned was to stay "on message." A candidate should have a few clear, simple things to say, and he should say them over and over. Every voter in Texas should know that George W. Bush was against crime, for education, for welfare reform, for reform of the legal system. "The four food groups," the Bush team called these points.

The George W. Bush campaign plane was named *Accountability One*. This name went with George W.'s message to the voters. When he announced that he was running for governor, he had said, "Our leaders should be judged by results, not by entertaining personalities or clever sound bites."

Former president Bush would have loved to campaign for his son, but they both knew that wasn't a good idea. It was hard enough to get voters to forget that George W. was his father's son. His *mother,* though—that was different.

Barbara Bush had been one of the most popular First Ladies of all time, and people admired her for her devotion to her family. Barbara helped campaign in Florida too, where George W.'s brother Jeb was running for governor. Their parents hoped both sons would win, of course. But they thought Jeb had a much better chance than George W. "You can't win," his mother told George when he first decided to run.

"You've been reading the *Washington Post* too long," George W. shot back. His point was that the national media, especially liberal newspapers like the *Post*, favored Ann Richards. But the media weren't going to elect the next governor of Texas. Texas voters would make that decision.

And George W. was determined to make contact with every voter he could, especially outside the big cities. He toured the state, stopping in small town after small town to shake hands. Since education was one of his issues, he would often visit schools.

At one elementary school some children got mixed up about George's last name and called him "Mr. Washington." George W. was delighted. He didn't want people to confuse him with his father, but he didn't mind being mistaken for our forefather George Washington!

As the campaign went on, Governor Richards and her supporters made jokes about George W.'s candidacy. They called him a lightweight, trading on his father's famous name. They scoffed at him for running for governor when he'd never held any kind of elected office before. "You can't be shaving one morning and look at yourself in the mirror and think, 'I'm so pretty I'll run for Governor,'" Ann Richards told Dallas reporters in March 1994.

Part of the Democratic strategy was to get George W. to lose his temper. Everyone knew he had a hot temper, and even his family and friends were sure he would crack sooner or later. But George W. kept his cool throughout the campaign.

Since Ann Richards was so well liked, George W. was careful not to attack her personally. He just kept campaigning hard, repeating his clear, simple points over and over. This was very much the way former president Ronald Reagan used to campaign, calm and cheerful and persistent.

In August 1994 Ann Richards and her team began to get worried. *She* attacked *him*. She called him "Shrub" and "Prince George," meaning that he expected to be elected just because his father had been president. She lost her temper, calling him a "jerk" in a public speech.

Three weeks before the election George W. Bush pulled ahead in the polls. In a televised debate, face-to-face with Ann Richards, he didn't lose his temper once.

Even people who had known George W. all his life, like his cousin Elsie Walker, couldn't believe how unruffled he appeared. Elsie sent Barbara Bush a flabbergasted telegram: WHAT HAS . . . WHAT DID HE DO?

On the morning of election day that November, George W. went to the polls in Dallas to vote. In his excitement, he left his identification—his driver's license and voter registration card—at home. The election judge assured him, with a straight face, that they could probably identify him.

By midafternoon the exit polls showed that Republican George W. Bush would win over Democrat Ann Richards by a comfortable margin. At ten o'clock that night Governor Richards called George W. to concede the election. CNN reported him the winner by the biggest margin in Texas in twenty years. When he got up to give his victory speech to his screaming supporters, George W. especially thanked "two Houstonians." He went on, "In case you weren't sure who I was talking about, one of them has real gray hair and wears pearls."

From Houston, George and Barbara Bush (the one with the gray hair and pearls) watched their first son on TV with tears of pride in their eyes. At the same time, they shed tears of hurt for their second son. Jeb Bush had just lost his race for governor in Florida.

Throughout most of the country, though, election day, 1994, was a day of triumph for the Republican Party. Congress was now controlled by the Republicans. Newt Gingrich, leader of the "Republican Revolution" against President Bill Clinton, would be the new Speaker of the House of Representatives.

In January 1995 George W. Bush was sworn in as the new governor of Texas. His whole family was there—Laura, the twins (now thirteen years old), his mother and father, and his brothers and sister. The Reverend Billy Graham gave the opening prayer.

At the end of the ceremony former president George Bush wiped a tear from his eye and hugged his granddaughter Jenna. "All Bushes cry easily when we're happy, or counting our blessings, or sad when one of us gets bruised or really hurt inside," he would explain a few years later. George W. Bush was now the first Republican governor of Texas since 1877.

George W. Bush moved his family again—this time to the white, pillared governor's mansion in Austin. He also moved into the governor's offices, along with his collection of 250 autographed baseballs. On the wall he hung a painting of a lone horseman riding up a steep, rocky trail. The painting, titled *A Charge to Keep,* had been inspired by one of George's favorite hymns. To George W. Bush, it summed up the rugged spirit of the Texas he loved.

Soon after taking office, George flew to Washington with Laura for the annual White House dinner for governors. It must have been hard for him to visit the White House, where just a few years earlier he had been comfortable as the president's son. At the reception he waited in the long line of governors to shake hands with President Bill Clinton—the man who had replaced his father. "I've never had to stand in line here before," he noted.

During 1995, his first year as governor of Texas, George worked hard to bring about the changes he had promised during his campaign. The governorship of Texas is not a powerful position, so he couldn't make many changes directly. But he was good at using the media to get publicity for his causes. And he could encourage and persuade the lawmakers—the state senators and state representatives—to take action.

This was the kind of work George did best: persuading and leading. He met weekly with Lieutenant Governor

Bob Bullock and Speaker of the House Pete Laney. He spent hours on the phone with legislators, reporters, lobbyists. He met with them personally. He sent them handwritten notes.

And all four of Governor Bush's "food groups" made progress. The Texas legislature took steps to give local school districts more control over public education. They passed laws providing stricter penalties for young criminals. And they encouraged business in Texas with laws protecting corporations from lawsuits. Texas lawmakers also enacted cuts in the state welfare system, and they passed laws requiring able-bodied people on welfare to work. At the same time, they changed regulations to encourage private charities to make up for the cuts in welfare. Governor Bush believed that faith-based charities, especially, could accomplish much more than government agencies.

Texas voters seemed happy with Governor Bush's accomplishments. By the end of his first year in office his approval ratings had risen from the fifties into the sixties.

The next year, 1996, President Bill Clinton and Vice President Al Gore ran for reelection. That summer Governor George W. Bush cochaired the Republican National Convention in San Diego. The convention nominated

Senator Bob Dole of Kansas as the Republican candidate for president. There was talk that Senator Dole might choose Governor Bush as his running mate.

But George W. knew this wasn't his time to run for vice president. As his father said, he needed to serve at least two terms as governor before he tried for national office. Meanwhile, the convention was wonderful national publicity for the young, good-looking, friendly Governor Bush.

The presidential race of 1996 was a close-fought campaign, but some political consultants thought that Senator Bob Dole was not the right person to run against Bill Clinton. Senator Dole had been a war hero in World War II, like former President Bush. And like President Bush, he had a hard time understanding how politics had changed.

In the new politics it was very important for a candidate to come across well on TV. Bill Clinton had always been good at this—he gave audiences the impression that he liked them and was glad to be talking with them. Bob Dole, on the other hand, sometimes came across as reserved and serious. On election day in November 1996 President Clinton was reelected.

But many Republicans were already looking ahead to the 2000 election. They had noticed that George W. Bush, like President Clinton, was relaxed and happy in front of TV cameras. Governor Bush understood how to appeal to moderate as well as conservative voters. Republican political consultants were already talking enthusiastically to reporters about George W. Bush and their hopes for 2000. They said, "He's our Clinton."

CHAPTER 13

MAKING THE BIG RUN

IN 1997 GEORGE W. BUSH AND HIS POLITICAL ADVISOR Karl Rove very quietly began planning a presidential campaign for the year 2000. That summer Governor Bush learned the results of a public opinion poll: He was already the first choice for the Republican nomination. For now, though, the strategy was *not* to talk publicly about the presidency in 2000. George W.'s father had given him sound advice: First, work hard to get reelected as governor.

But in his quest for reelection George W. faced some difficulties. During the spring of 1997 Governor Bush had tried to get the legislature to pass a large property tax cut, but he finally had to compromise on a smaller tax cut. He also tried to get approval from Washington, D.C., to let private companies, instead of state agencies, run Texas programs for the poor and elderly. But the Clinton administration refused permission.

That fall Governor Bush was faced with a different kind of problem: a condemned prisoner named Karla Faye Tucker. As a teenager thirteen years before, Tucker had committed a grisly murder. While in prison, she had converted to Christianity and since then had been working to help other prisoners change their lives.

Amid a storm of publicity Karla Faye Tucker was scheduled to be executed at the beginning of 1998. The TV program *60 Minutes* broadcast a story on her case. Christian conservatives, led by Pat Robertson, publicly begged the governor to grant a reprieve. Pope John Paul II wrote a letter to the governor. One of George's own daughters announced to him that she was against capital punishment.

But Governor Bush knew that Tucker was guilty of murder. He was convinced that she had received a fair trial and that her case had been reviewed completely. It would be wrong, he believed, for him to grant the reprieve. On February 3, 1998, Karla Faye Tucker was executed at the state prison in Huntsville. Governor Bush and his staff sat in his office listening to the description of the execution by lethal injection. He said, "I felt like a huge piece of concrete was crushing me as I waited."

In spite of some harsh criticism, Governor Bush's approval rating was high among most Texas voters. His popularity at the beginning of the 1998 campaign was 76 percent. He had followed through on all four of his campaign promises: to reform education, to make the juvenile justice system more effective, to reduce business's liability in lawsuits, and to reform welfare.

Lieutenant Governor Bob Bullock, although he was a Democrat, actually contributed money to George W.'s 1998 campaign. It didn't make good sense, Bullock explained, to try to remove a successful governor from office. And so it was a sure thing that in November, George W. Bush would become the first governor of Texas to be elected to two four-year terms in a row.

In Florida, George's brother Jeb was running for governor again. Of course George wanted his brother to win. But besides that, it would be good for Republicans in general if Jeb Bush became governor in 1998. It would mean that Florida, long a Democratic state, was becoming Republican. And Jeb's triumph would help Governor Bush's chances in the 2000 presidential election.

There had already been a good sign. In May 1998 a nationwide public opinion poll in *USA Today* had asked voters whom they would vote for if the 2000 election were held right then. The results showed that George W. Bush would beat Vice President Gore.

That November, Governor George W. Bush was reelected by a landslide. In his victory speech he was delighted to include a message to Jeb, now the governor-elect of Florida: "Good going, brother." In this same speech George described himself with words he would use over and over during the next two years: "compassionate conservative." Governor Bush believed it was possible to be financially conservative in government and still help people in need.

George W.'s father was overjoyed to have two sons as governors. At the same time, he was concerned about the next political step for his firstborn son. He knew that the minute the 1998 election was over, the pressure would be on Governor Bush as a presidential candidate. From personal experience former president Bush knew how brutal that pressure could be. "He is strong, though," he wrote a friend about his first son. "Tough enough, too, to withstand the pressure."

President Bush relished the idea that if his son were elected, it would be a historic moment. In American history the only time a son had followed a father into the White House was in 1825. That was the year that John Quincy Adams, son of John Adams, became president.

Actually, George W. wasn't sure that running for president in 2000 was the right thing to do. He *liked* being governor of Texas, and his second term would last through 2002. More important, he was concerned about his daughters, Jenna and Barbara. They were teenagers, and living in the spotlight of a presidential campaign would be especially hard for them.

But George knew that if he didn't run in 2000, he might never get another chance. He felt he had a special gift to bring to the presidency: an ability to lead and to help opposing groups get along and work with each other. So he listened carefully at a prayer service before his gubernatorial inauguration in January 1999.

Make the most of every moment, said the preacher. Rise to the challenge. People are "starved for leaders who have ethical and moral courage." Afterward George's mother told him, "He was talking to you." It was time to start working in earnest on George W. Bush's campaign for president.

The Bush team assumed, from the beginning, that Vice President Al Gore would be the Democratic candidate. Al Gore might benefit from Bill Clinton's popularity, as Vice President George Bush had benefited from Ronald Reagan's popularity in the election of 1988. On the other hand, Bill Clinton had been disgraced the previous year—and his disgrace might rub off on Vice President Gore.

Early in 1998 President Clinton had been accused of having an improper relationship with a former White House intern, Monica Lewinsky. The scandal had grown all year, until the House of Representatives voted to impeach the president. Although he was eventually acquitted, many voters were disgusted with President Clinton's personal behavior.

Meanwhile, Governor Bush had a solid reputation as a loving family man. George W. freely admitted that he *used* to indulge in wild partying. "When I was young and irresponsible," he told a reporter, "I was young and irresponsible. I changed when I married my wife and I changed when I had children."

Early in the presidential race it was clear that Governor Bush had a lot going for him. In the first month of fund-raising he received $7.5 million for his campaign.

George W. Bush on the shoulders of his father, George H. W. Bush, on the campus of Yale University in 1947.

George W. Bush in an F102 fighter jet while in the Texas Air National Guard.

George H. W. Bush announces his candidacy for the Republican presidential nomination in 1979.

George and Laura Bush watch a Texas Rangers baseball game in Plano, Texas, in 1990.

George and Laura Bush await the results of the 1994 election for Texas governor.

George W. Bush and his twin daughters, Barbara and Jenna, on November 8, 1994, election day for the governor of Texas.

Republican presidential nominee George W. Bush and running mate Dick Cheney campaigning in Pittsburgh, Pennsylvania.

George W. Bush awaits the final results of the presidential election inside the governor's mansion.

President George W. Bush and Secretary of Defense Donald Rumsfeld visit the Pentagon after the 9/11 terrorist attacks.

President George W. Bush talks with retired firefighter Bob Beckwith at the site of the World Trade Center disaster in New York City in September 2001.

A U.S. Marine watches as a statue of Saddam Hussein falls in Firdaus Square in Baghdad, Iraq.

Former Iraqi dictator Saddam Hussein at his tribunal hearing in Baghdad, Iraq.

Condoleezza Rice is sworn in as secretary of state by U.S. Supreme Court Justice
Ruth Bader Ginsburg, in 2005.

George W. Bush, surrounded by Dick Cheney, Condoleezza Rice, Donald Rumsfeld, and senior administration officials, after meeting about defense and foreign policy at Bush's ranch in Crawford, Texas.

Aerial view of Hurricane Katrina's massive flooding in New Orleans, Louisiana, in September 2005.

In postwar Iraq's first full-term parliamentary elections, in December 2004, two Iraqi women show their inked fingers after voting.

The financial crisis affected American homeowners, who owed more on their mortgages than their homes were worth. Many couldn't afford the payments and had to give up their houses.

President Bush and leaders of Congress as he signs the Economic Stimulus Act of 2008 in the East Room of the White House.

President Bush and President-Elect Barack Obama in the Oval Office at the White House, six days after Obama became the first African-American in history to win the presidency in November 2008.

Former President Bush and Laura Bush, greeted by well-wishers as they return home to Texas in January 2009.

The Republican Party had lost its focus since the days of President Ronald Reagan, and many Republicans felt that George W. Bush was just the candidate to pull the party back together. People liked being around George W. because he was upbeat and energetic—and because *he* liked being around people. His enthusiasm was contagious, whether it was about a grand stickball tournament in 1964 or about the presidential campaign of 2000.

The Bush team decided to emphasize what George W. Bush could do for American education as president. In Texas he had backed statewide tests in reading and math for all students in the third through eighth grades. Each school district had to make progress in its students' performance or else lose funding. As a result, test scores had gone up—especially for African-American and Latino children.

The Bush team was aware that many people thought of Republicans as the "mean" party—the ones who wanted to cut benefits for poor people while helping big business. George W. Bush set out to change this impression with his slogan of "compassionate conservatism." His idea was that the president could encourage nongovernment programs, especially faith-based programs, to help people turn their lives around. He would fight poverty this way, not with big, expensive programs run from Washington, D.C.

To let voters get to know him better, and to communicate his philosophy of government, George W. Bush wrote *A Charge to Keep*, published in 1999. This book is a collection of stories from Bush's life, beginning in his childhood, as well as explanations of his political views.

George W. Bush's friendly, unpretentious manner appealed to a wide range of voters, not just die-hard Republicans. In Texas, Governor Bush was popular with many Latino voters, although Latinos had traditionally voted Democratic. Republicans often criticized immigrants—and in Texas *immigrants* usually meant Latino people. But George W. made friends with important Latino politicians, and he even spoke Spanish with a decent accent. Carlos Ramirez, the mayor of the key Latino city of El Paso, had endorsed Governor Bush in the 1998 gubernatorial election.

On the other hand, some critics felt that George W. Bush was not serious enough, or experienced enough, to be president. He had never held a national office. He had never served in a war, and he had no experience with foreign policy. During the winter of 1998–99 Governor Bush's most serious rival for the Republican nomination turned out to be Senator John McCain of Arizona. Senator McCain was a Vietnam War hero, with permanent injuries from his years as a prisoner of war. In Congress, McCain had been a leader in national-defense and foreign-policy matters.

In the primary elections in the spring of 2000 it seemed at first that John McCain might actually win the Republican nomination. But by the end of March it was clear that no one could beat George W. Bush. Senator McCain announced that he was dropping out of the race. At the same time, in the Democratic primary elections, Vice President Al Gore emerged as the winner. So the race for president in 2000 would be between George W. Bush and Al Gore, as the Bush team had thought from the beginning.

Vice President Gore would be a tough opponent. Becoming president had been his lifelong ambition, and he had already worked in national government for twenty-three years. George W. had held only one public office, governor of Texas. Al Gore studied hard to make himself an expert on difficult subjects, such as climate change and international trade. Governor Bush tended instead to surround himself with knowledgeable people and trust them to keep him well informed.

But George W. knew that in some ways it was an advantage not to be an experienced Washington politician. Many voters felt that Washington politicians spent more time fighting with one another than working for the people.

As a candidate, George W. Bush had one big advantage over both his father and Al Gore: In front of TV cameras, or speaking to a crowd, he came across as friendly and relaxed. Like former President Ronald Reagan, he seemed cheerful and optimistic. George W. Bush gave audiences the impression that he liked them, and they tended to like him back. In May 2000 a *New York Times*/CBS News poll showed that voters liked George W. Bush better than Al Gore. They also thought Governor Bush was a more commanding leader. Nearly half of all voters expected Governor Bush to win in November.

Al Gore, on the other hand, had never really enjoyed campaigning. In the spotlight he was often stiff and awkward. He sometimes bored audiences with too many facts. And he had another disadvantage—although he was devoted to his wife, Tipper, many people associated him with the scandal of President Clinton's impeachment.

Now that George W. Bush was sure to be nominated at the Republican convention, he needed to pick a running mate. He asked Dick Cheney to lead the search. Cheney had been a congressman from Wyoming, and then he had served as President Bush's secretary of defense. For the last few years he had been an oil company executive. His politics were solidly conservative, and he had a calm, low-key manner.

Just before the Republican National Convention in Philadelphia at the end of July, Governor Bush announced his decision. Realizing that the best man for the job was the one conducting the search, George decided his running mate would be Dick Cheney himself. They would make a good balance, since Cheney was experienced in national politics and foreign affairs. He was only a few years older than George W. Bush, but he was as dignified as George W. was peppy and casual.

On the first night of the Republican convention Laura Bush gave the opening speech. She had come a long way since her stumbling speech on the courthouse steps in Muleshoe in 1978. Now she was poised, warm, and humorous as she talked about her husband.

Laura told the audience that, as a former teacher, she was proud of the education reforms Governor Bush had supported in Texas. She reminded them of the "fabulous results" of those reforms. She explained the Reading First initiative George wanted for the whole country, "to make sure every child in every neighborhood can read on grade level by the end of the third grade." Laura also mentioned George's record, as governor of Texas, of working with both Democrats and Republicans "to get things done." She added, "He sets a tone that's very different from the bitterness and the division that too often characterize Washington, D.C."

On the last night of the convention George gave his speech accepting the Republican nomination for president. Working with his speechwriter, George had made sure that his language was simple and clear, and that the speech was not too long. He had been rewriting and practicing the speech for several weeks because a lot depended on it. Although he would be speaking to the Republicans in the convention hall, the most important audience was the voters all across the nation watching him on TV. This was his moment to introduce himself to the whole country and show them that he could be their leader.

One of the speakers who came before Governor Bush that night was his nephew George P. Bush, son of

Jeb Bush and his Mexican wife, Columba. George P. gave his speech partly in Spanish, reminding Latino voters of Governor Bush's good relations with Latinos in Texas. Then George W. Bush stepped up to give his speech. Nearby, other members of his family—his mother and father, Laura, and his daughters, Barbara and Jenna—sat beaming at him.

Clearly and simply George laid out the differences between him and Al Gore. He emphasized that Vice President Gore was part of the Clinton administration, with all its disappointments. "They had their chance," he said over and over. "They have not led. We will."

George's speech was a success. Polls right after the convention showed George W. Bush leading Al Gore by more than ten points. But Governor Bush and his team knew that polls didn't mean that much at this stage of the campaign.

George was right not to get too excited about the polls, because the numbers continued to go back and forth. After the Democratic National Convention in mid-August it was Al Gore's turn to enjoy a postconvention rebound. Then in September, when George appeared on *Oprah,* his numbers rose.

During the last month of the campaign, the two presidential candidates met three times for official debates. The first debate was held on October 3 at the University of Massachusetts in Boston. Some forty-six million TV viewers watched the two men standing at podiums, answering questions from moderator Jim Lehrer. Vice President Gore's answers showed off his knowledge, especially of foreign policy. But he made a bad impression with many viewers by acting aggressive. Several times he interrupted Governor Bush and the moderator, or sighed loudly and shook his head while George was speaking.

George, as in his debate with Ann Richards in 1994, stayed calm under attack. If he were elected president, he explained, he would do what he had done as governor of Texas: He would solve problems. He would bring people together. He would lead in a positive way.

George held off criticizing Vice President Gore personally until the end of the debate. Then he said he was "discouraged" and "disappointed" by the vice president's fund-raising behavior. "We need to have a new look about how we conduct ourselves in office."

Polls taken afterward showed that the debate didn't change the way voters thought about the candidates. The race was still much too close to call. In fact, it was the closest presidential race since 1960, when John F. Kennedy beat Richard Nixon by a whisker. But George was out campaigning the next morning, not waiting to see the poll results. He knew there was a month of hard work ahead before "Reality Day"—the Bush name for election day, the day the voters would make their final choice.

CHAPTER 14

A HAIRSBREADTH VICTORY

BY MONDAY, NOVEMBER 6, THE DAY BEFORE THE election, the race was closer than ever. Governor Bush and his team remained upbeat, but George knew no one could say what would happen tomorrow—Reality Day 2000. He needed to make a last big effort in the "battleground" states where the election could be decided.

George had spent Sunday campaigning in Florida, which was in danger of going for Al Gore in spite of George's brother Jeb Bush being its governor. On Monday, George began a final sixteen-hour push with a rally in Tennessee. Even though Tennessee was Al Gore's home state, George had a good chance of winning there. Afterward he flew to Wisconsin and Iowa—two important swing states—and finished the hard day's campaigning in Arkansas, President Clinton's home state. He returned to the governor's mansion in Austin, Texas, late that night.

Early on November 7, election day, George went to the polls to cast his vote. That evening he and his family—including his mother and father and brother Jeb—were eating dinner at an Austin restaurant when they heard some bad news. The television networks had announced that the state of Florida had gone to Vice President Gore. The Bush family quickly left for the privacy of the governor's mansion and watched the election returns in the upstairs living room.

Jeb Bush was sure the networks were mistaken about Florida. In fact, a few hours later, the networks changed their minds and announced that Florida was too close to call. As it turned out, this news was extremely important because of the mechanics behind how America elects its presidents.

The president of the United States is not elected by the *popular* vote, which is the total of all votes cast throughout the country. Instead, our president is actually elected by the state-by-state *electoral* vote. The Constitution provides that each state has a certain number of electoral votes, which equals that state's number of U.S. Representatives (different for each state) plus the number of senators (always two). Alaska, a state with a small population, has only 3 electoral votes, but heavily populated Florida has 25. The winner of the most votes cast in each state wins that state's electoral votes.

Nationwide, the total number of electoral votes in the election of 2000 was 538. The candidate who won a majority—270 electoral votes or more—would win the presidency. By the end of Reality Day 2000, with Florida still undecided, Governor Bush had won 246 electoral votes, and Vice President Gore had won 255. Interestingly, George had won both Al Gore's home state of Tennessee and Bill Clinton's home state of Arkansas. Like Florida, New Mexico (5 electoral votes) and Oregon (7 electoral votes) were also too close to call, but at this point they didn't matter. Whoever won Florida's 25 electoral votes would win the election.

Finally, around one o'clock Wednesday morning, November 8, the networks made a new announcement: George had *won* Florida. George W. Bush now had enough electoral votes to become the next president of the United States. Vice President Gore called George to concede the election.

Less than two hours later, as George was about to

leave the governor's mansion to give his victory speech, Al Gore called again. He wanted to take back his concession. Florida officials had just announced that Governor Bush led the vice president by only 1,200 votes. With such a close election, a statewide recount was necessary. Instead of celebrating with a victory party, George had to wait while Florida began to recount its votes.

On Tuesday evening, November 14—a full week after election day—the official recount tally was announced. George had indeed won the state of Florida. His lead was now a mere 300 votes, but he still had won.

This was not the end of the election, though. Absentee ballots still needed to be counted, and the Democrats demanded another recount of the votes in Broward, Miami-Dade, and Palm Beach counties, this time by hand. The voting in these counties had been done on punch-card ballots, and the machines that counted the ballots sometimes made mistakes. If the voter had not completely punched out the "chad"—the little square of paper indicating a vote—the machine might fail to count that vote. In a hand count, the human election workers could see if the chad was hanging (partly punched out) and know what that vote was meant to be.

Because counting by hand would take much longer than by machine, Vice President Gore claimed that more time was needed beyond November 14. But Florida Secretary of State Kathleen Harris refused to change the date. The Gore team appealed her decision to the Florida Supreme Court, and the court ruled to extend the deadline to November 26 and to include the hand recounts. Not wanting the recounts to drag on any longer, the Bush team then appealed to the U.S. Supreme Court to overturn the Florida Supreme Court's ruling.

The U.S. Supreme Court case over the deadline would not be heard until December 1. So on the evening of November 26, Florida Secretary of State Harris, who was the person authorized in the state of Florida to declare the winner of Florida's presidential election, certified the votes. She did not include the results of the incomplete hand count in Palm Beach County, and election officials in Miami-Dade County had given up their hand count. Since George W. Bush was the winner—now by 537 votes—she announced that Florida's 25 electoral votes would therefore go to him.

This certification was important because it gave Governor Bush's victory some official status. It would be harder for the Gore team to get the courts to *overturn* the certification than it had been to *prevent* certification. Also, in the mind of the public, certification moved Governor Bush closer to the presidency.

Shortly afterward, George made a public announcement at the Texas State Capitol in Austin. His quiet words were far from the victory speech he had planned almost three weeks earlier. "Secretary Cheney and I are honored and humbled to have won the state of Florida, which gives us the needed electoral votes to win the election. We will therefore undertake the responsibility of preparing to serve as America's next president and vice president."

But still Vice President Gore did not concede. Only a few hundred votes separated him from the presidency. He believed he might well win if the hand counts were completed in Palm Beach and Miami-Dade counties and those results included in the Florida total. The Gore lawyers appealed to a Florida circuit court (which is the court just below the Florida Supreme Court) to order the hand counts completed. They also fought hard before the U.S. Supreme Court to let stand the Florida Supreme Court's ruling to extend the deadline.

On December 4, four weeks after the election, the

U.S. Supreme Court and the Florida circuit court both announced their decisions. The Supreme Court simply sent the case back to the Florida Supreme Court, asking it to clarify why it had extended the deadline and to reconsider that course of action. But the Florida circuit court refused outright to order the hand count requested by the Gore team.

Governor Bush and his team thought this was only right. They had believed all along that hand counts couldn't be completely fair. Vote-counting machines might make mistakes, but at least those mistakes were impartial. Also, in hand counts there were no clear rules for deciding what the voter had meant. If the chad in a punch-card ballot wasn't punched out but there was a "dimple" in it, did that mean that the voter had tried to punch it out? Or did it just mean that the voter had rested the stylus on the chad and then decided against that vote?

In a news conference, Governor Bush was careful not to sound triumphant. "I'm grateful that the court made the decision that it made," he said. When asked if he didn't think it was high time for Vice President Gore to concede, George answered, "That's a very difficult decision for anybody to make. I do believe I have won this election.

I believe that I won it on the first count and on the second count and on the third count. But the vice president's going to have to make the decisions that he thinks are necessary. And I know that the interests of the country will be important in his decision making, just like it would be in mine."

Vice President Gore's decision was to appeal the Florida circuit court's ruling to the Florida Supreme Court. On December 8, the Florida Supreme Court ruled that the hand counts of the votes must continue. Immediately the Bush team's lawyers appealed to the U.S. Supreme Court to overturn the Florida Supreme Court and to stop the hand counts at least until the U.S. Supreme Court ruled on this case.

The back-and-forth of the legal cases was like a dizzying game of Ping-Pong, with the presidency depending on each stroke. But George W. Bush stayed calm. He believed that it was only a matter of time before his victory finally became official. He had already started working on his transition from president-elect to president. He sent his transition team, headed by Dick Cheney, to Washington, D.C., and he continued to choose the members of his cabinet.

All this time it seemed as if the whole country were holding its breath, waiting to know who the next president would be. Nothing like this had happened since 1876, when it appeared that Republican Rutherford B. Hayes had won the White House from Democrat Samuel J. Tilden by only one electoral vote. The Democrats contested the election, and the deadlock went on for months. The election was finally settled by Congress—with great difficulty—only three days before Hayes's inauguration in 1877.

Luckily, the election of 2000 didn't stretch out into January 2001. As the Bush lawyers had asked, the U.S. Supreme Court ordered the hand counting halted while it considered the Florida Supreme Court's last decision. While this wasn't the final decision, the Bush team took it as a very good sign. And then on December 12, exactly five weeks after election day, the U.S. Supreme Court ruled that the hand counting must stop permanently.

The majority of the Supreme Court justices agreed that the Florida Supreme Court, in ordering the hand counts, had not made sure that they would be done according to a fair, uniform standard in every county. It also decided that it was impossible to come up with a fair *and* quick way of counting the contested votes. Time was important because all arguments about the outcome of the vote were supposed to be settled by December 12—the same day as the Supreme Court's decision. In other words, there was no time left for any more recounts.

With the Supreme Court's decision, Vice President Gore's last hope to win the presidency was dashed. The following evening he gave a televised speech conceding the election, this time for good. Al Gore would no longer contest the fact that Florida's 25 electoral votes belonged to George W. Bush.

George had won the presidency, but his victory was one of the narrowest in American history. And the drawn-out struggle after the election had underlined the divisions in the country. The U.S. Congress—both the Senate and the House of Representatives—was now almost evenly split between Democrats and Republicans. But George was confident he could handle this difficult presidency, because he had a record of working well with Democrats in Texas. Ever since he was a boy, he'd had a talent for getting along with other people—for persuading and leading. Throughout the recount in Florida, George had stressed the importance of bringing the nation together once the election finally ended.

An hour after Al Gore finished his speech, Governor Bush spoke from the Texas State Capitol. Enthusiastic applause greeted him as he was introduced by Speaker of the Texas House of Representatives Pete Laney, a Democrat. George looked very happy but calm as he spoke: "I have a lot to be thankful for tonight. I'm thankful for America and thankful that we were able to resolve our electoral differences in a peaceful way."

In his speech on the night he finally became president-elect, George emphasized his intention to "move beyond the bitterness and partisanship of the recent past." He explained, "Tonight I chose to speak from the chamber of the Texas House of Representatives because it has been a home to bipartisan cooperation. Here in a place where Democrats have the majority, Republicans and Democrats have worked together to do what is right for the people we represent."

This was the spirit of cooperation that George wanted to bring to Washington, D.C. "Our nation must rise above a house divided. Americans share hopes and goals and values far more important than any political disagreements. . . . Our votes may differ, but not our hopes." He pointed out the "remarkable consensus about the important issues

138

before us: excellent schools, retirement and health security, tax relief, a strong military, a more civil society."

In the conclusion of his speech, George W. Bush told the audience in the hall and all the Americans watching him on TV, "The presidency is more than an honor. It is more than an office. It is a charge to keep, and I will give it my all." On January 20, 2001, that charge would begin— George W. Bush would be inaugurated as the forty-third president of the United States.

CHAPTER 15

"AMERICA IS UNDER ATTACK"

AFTER SUCH A NARROW VICTORY IN THE ELECTION of 2000, most Americans expected George W. Bush's administration to get off to a slow, cautious start. At the beginning of a new president's term, time is often wasted just in getting used to Washington politics. This had happened to the last president, Bill Clinton. But George W. Bush and his staff hit the ground running.

President George W. Bush had a head start because of the people he chose to work with him. Vice President Richard Chency, as well as many of the others in the new administration, had years of experience in national politics. Secretary of Defense Donald Rumsfeld served in the Ford, Reagan, and first Bush administrations. Colin Powell, the new secretary of state, was a four-star general. He had been a national security advisor to President Ronald Reagan, and he was chairman of the Joint Chiefs of Staff during George H. W. Bush's presidency. National Security Advisor Condoleezza Rice had also worked in the first President Bush's administration, and she advised George W. Bush on national security during his campaign for president.

As President George W. Bush began his first year in office, he kept in mind the way Ronald Reagan, president from 1981 to 1989, had pursued his goals. President Reagan and his staff never lost sight of what they wanted to accomplish: Reduce the size of the government. Cut taxes. Forcefully defend American interests in the rest of the world.

George W. Bush's political aims were much like Ronald Reagan's, and he wanted to pursue them in a similarly focused way. Bush was determined to achieve two main goals. The first was to cut taxes. President Bush and his advisors thought that reducing taxes would be good for businesses and result in more jobs for Americans. The president also felt it was only fair for people to keep more of the money they earned instead of paying it to the government as taxes.

Critics of the new administration said that this tax cut plan would help rich Americans more than poor and middle-income Americans. They also feared that without

141

the money earned from taxes, the federal government would fall dangerously into debt. That is, the government would have to either borrow money or cut programs to meet its expenses. In spite of these objections, in May 2001 Congress approved a large tax cut: $1.35 trillion over ten years. This was not as deep a tax cut as the one President Bush had asked for, but it was still an impressive victory.

George W. Bush's second goal was to reform American education. He worked on this issue with Democrats and Republicans alike, just as he had promised during the campaign of 2000. President Bush joined forces with Senator Edward Kennedy, a Democrat from Massachusetts, on education reform. Senator Kennedy had long been regarded by many Republicans as a political archenemy. But now he supported President Bush in passing a law, the No Child Left Behind Act, that required public schools to meet high standards.

On some other issues the Bush administration was not so successful in its early days. President Bush wanted to open the Arctic National Wildlife Refuge in Alaska to drilling for oil and natural gas. The president argued that Alaskan oil would reduce American dependence on foreign supplies. But too many senators were concerned that such drilling would harm the environment, and President Bush could not get this energy plan passed.

George W. Bush was also eager to encourage faith-based charities, just as he had while governor of Texas. President Bush felt his Christian faith had changed his life for the better, and he believed that religious groups could be a powerful force in solving national problems. For instance, he thought they could do a better job than government agencies in treating drug addiction and providing child welfare. But many Americans were wary of giving government money to religious groups. And many religious groups were wary of taking government money for their work, fearing that the government would try to control them.

By the summer of 2001 the Bush administration seemed to have lost some momentum. A Republican senator had left the party and became an Independent. Now the Democrats controlled the Senate. It seemed that it would be much more difficult for President Bush to lead the country in the direction he wanted to go.

On September 11, 2001, everything changed—for George W. Bush and for the country. The president's day began on a cheerful note, as he visited an elementary school in Sarasota, Florida. He sat on a stool in front of a sign that read, READING MAKES A COUNTRY GREAT! and listened to a class of second-graders reading out loud. He planned to speak to reporters afterward about his education policy.

Soon after he entered the classroom President Bush was told by his advisor Karl Rove that a plane had crashed into the north tower of the World Trade Center in New York City. This was a serious disaster, but at first it seemed that the crash was a freak accident. The president decided to continue with the classroom visit. Then, as the second-grade lesson went on, Chief of Staff Andrew Card whispered in the president's ear.

Card's news was very bad. Another plane had crashed into the south tower of the World Trade Center. The first crash was clearly no accident. "America is under attack," said the chief of staff. It was a national emergency.

President Bush sat with the children for a few more minutes as they read a story titled "The Pet Goat." But he must have been thinking of much more serious matters. For the first time since the British burned Washington, D.C., during the War of 1812, an enemy had struck a serious blow on the continental United States. In some ways this was more terrifying than the attack on Pearl Harbor at the beginning of World War II.

Outside the Florida school President Bush gave his press conference, but not about education, as he planned. He knew that all over the country Americans were staring at their TV screens, watching in horror as the hijacked jet airplanes crashed into the towers, smoke and flames billowed out, and the buildings collapsed. Americans needed to see the president of the United States in public and hear him speak about the disaster.

The president told the country of the attacks on New York, and he promised that the United States would hunt down and punish those responsible. Then, on the advice of the Secret Service, he boarded his plane, Air Force One. He would remain out of harm's way and not return to Washington yet.

In flight President Bush received more grim news. The Pentagon in Washington, headquarters for the Department of Defense, had been hit by a third suicide plane. And a fourth hijacked jetliner had also been seen heading for Washington. This plane was probably meant to destroy the White House or the Capitol Building. But after a struggle between the hijackers and passengers, the fourth plane crashed into a field in southwestern Pennsylvania.

"We're at war," President Bush told his aides. He spoke by telephone to Vice President Cheney, who was in a tunnel under the White House. Both the vice president and the Secret Service urged the president not to return to Washington yet. They feared more attacks to come, including attempts to kill the president. So Air Force One flew on, first to Louisiana, then to Nebraska.

The Secret Service's mission to always protect the president was more urgent than ever. Americans were already stunned and frightened by the destruction of the Twin Towers. If the attackers succeeded in killing the president, the country would be thrown into panic.

But President Bush became more and more concerned about how his absence from Washington would affect the morale of the nation. George W. Bush had confidence in Vice President Richard Cheney and had given him an unusual amount of responsibility and influence. But there was only one president, and George W. Bush felt that the American people needed to see him leading the government, in spite of the disaster.

At the end of that fateful day he insisted on returning to the White House. The millions of Americans glued to their TV sets saw their leader fly in the presidential helicopter from Andrews Air Force Base, land on the South Lawn of the White House, and enter the Oval Office.

That evening President Bush addressed the nation. "The search is underway for those who are behind these evil acts," he said. "We will make no distinction between the terrorists who committed these acts and those who harbor them."

Earlier, while George W. Bush was still in Nebraska, Director of the Central Intelligence Agency George Tenet had informed him who the enemy was. Only al-Qaeda, a worldwide terrorist organization led by an exiled Saudi named Osama bin Laden, was powerful enough to accomplish such devastating attacks.

A few days later, President Bush called for a national day of mourning. He and his wife, Laura Bush, as well as former presidents Bill Clinton, George H.W. Bush, Jimmy Carter, Gerald Ford, and their wives, attended a televised service at the National Cathedral in Washington. They led the nation in grieving for the nearly three thousand people killed in the attacks of September 11.

In the days that followed, President Bush expressed Americans' anger as well as their grief. He visited Ground Zero, the site of the destroyed World Trade Center in

New York City. Standing amid the smoking rubble, George W. Bush gave an impromptu speech.

President Bush was given a bullhorn to speak with since no microphone was available. When a rescue worker in the audience shouted, "I can't hear you," the president shouted back, "I can hear *you*. The rest of the world hears you. And the people who knocked these buildings down will hear all of us soon!"

On September 20, George W. Bush gave a formal speech to Congress. It was also a speech to the nation and to the world. He announced that the terrorist organization al-Qaeda was responsible for the attacks on New York and Washington. In response, the United States was launching a war on terror. The U.S. demanded that the Taliban, the government of Afghanistan, hand over Osama bin Laden and the other al-Qaeda leaders who were hiding there.

In the same speech, President Bush announced the creation of an additional governmental department: the Office of Homeland Security. This new cabinet position underlined the importance of protecting the United States from would-be attackers. The whole country would have to get used to stricter security measures.

George W. and Laura Bush themselves had to live with

tighter than usual security as well. In the White House, they were at the very center of a target for terrorists. The Bushes lay awake at night, hearing the roar of Combat Air Patrol planes circling the capital. The usual public tours of the White House had to be canceled, and the mansion seemed lonely without the constant stream of visitors. The Bushes didn't talk to each other about it, but they were both grimly aware that snipers were stationed on the roof of the White House to watch the grounds for terrorists.

In the midst of all the fear and grief, there was one positive outcome of the September 11 tragedy: Americans reacted by pulling together. The bickering between Republicans and Democrats seemed unimportant compared with the country's safety. On a visit to Congress George W. Bush publicly hugged his fierce political enemy Tom Daschle, leader of the Democrats in the Senate. Around the country the American flag flew from highway overpass bridges, appeared in car windows, and sprouted on lawns and T-shirts of conservatives and liberals alike.

President Bush's approval rating soared to 90 percent, an all-time record for any president. The Senate and the House of Representatives passed a joint resolution giving the president wider powers to use force without consulting Congress first. This resolution gave President Bush the authority to send U.S. troops to hunt down those responsible for the September 11 attacks.

Other countries around the world, even those whose leaders had previously criticized President Bush, sympathized with the U.S. They condemned the terrorists and offered help to Americans. The United Nations Security Council immediately passed a resolution condemning the September 11 attacks. All over the world millions of people gathered at vigils and rallies in support of the United States.

In Afghanistan the Taliban government refused to hand over Osama bin Laden, or any other members of al-Qaeda. As a response, the United States and its allies launched attacks on Afghanistan in October 2001. Many countries, including Britain, Germany, and France, took part. By Thanksgiving the Taliban was defeated and deposed from power, and the U.S. and its allies worked to set up a new government in Afghanistan. Osama bin Laden, however, had not been captured or killed. In fact, he continued to send messages to the world through videotapes played on the Arabic news network Al Jazeera.

Meanwhile, what could be done about terrorism at

home? The men who hijacked the four planes on September 11 had come to the United States without being detected. They had lived here for several years, and they had even learned to fly commercial jets in this country. It seemed especially horrifying that these terrorists had been hiding in plain sight for so long without being discovered. In October 2001 Congress passed the USA Patriot Act, giving the government more power to investigate individuals.

Under the Patriot Act, Attorney General John Ashcroft had the right to arrest and imprison any suspected terrorists without a trial or access to a lawyer. He could order a library or bookstore to hand over the records of the books a person had checked out or bought. Security in public buildings became tighter, including searches of handbags and backpacks. At airports, travelers became used to taking off their shoes and having their luggage searched before they boarded a plane.

Americans were still badly frightened; many of them were afraid to travel and wondered where and when the next terrorist attack would hit. Deadly anthrax bacteria sent through the U.S. mail killed five people during the fall of 2001, and no one knew who was responsible. Before

September 11 Americans had been very concerned with the economy, but now they cared more about public safety. They looked to the president to protect them.

At the end of January 2002 President Bush gave his annual State of the Union address. In Bush's War on Terror, the U.S. would focus on three countries: Iran, Iraq, and North Korea. He said they formed an "axis of evil."

Many people were surprised that the president linked these three countries, since Iraq and Iran had been bitter enemies for years, and neither of them had close connections with North Korea. But President Bush explained that Iran, Iraq, and North Korea were especially dangerous in the same ways: All three had governments that controlled their people by force, all were determined to build weapons of mass destruction, and all provided arms to terrorists. President Bush made it clear, however, that he believed Saddam Hussein's regime in Iraq was the greatest danger to peace.

By November 2002 the congressional elections still showed the effects of the attacks of September 11, 2001. Usually, by the middle of a president's first term, his popularity with the voters has slumped. At midterm the president's party usually loses elections in Congress. But

George W. Bush, seen as the firm, decisive leader the country needed after September 11, still had a high approval rating with the voters. In the fall of 2002 the president used his popularity to campaign for Republican candidates to Congress.

In the November elections the president's work for his party paid off. Republicans strengthened their lead in the House of Representatives and took control of the Senate away from the Democrats. With this new political power President Bush proposed and won a second large tax cut in 2003, in spite of the fact that the deficit was growing. George W. Bush believed that his tax cuts would help the country in the end, and that most Americans supported the cuts. He also believed that Congress and the American public would support his intention to remove Saddam Hussein from power in Iraq.

CHAPTER 16

THE WAR IN IRAQ

EVEN BEFORE SEPTEMBER 11 GEORGE W. BUSH AND his advisors had been sure that Iraq posed a serious threat to the United States. The dictator of Iraq, Saddam Hussein, was a sworn enemy of the U.S. During President George H. W. Bush's administration, the U.S. and its allies had driven Iraqi invaders out of neighboring Kuwait. They also forced Iraq to agree to weapons inspections by the United Nations.

Saddam Hussein, however, did his best to disrupt the inspections, and in 1998 he finally ordered the UN inspectors to leave the country. It was impossible to tell if Iraq had destroyed all its weapons of mass destruction. There was strong suspicion that Iraq was secretly developing chemical weapons, like the poison gas Saddam Hussein had used on Iraqi Kurds, or biological weapons, such as the deadly anthrax bacteria. And now President Bush, Vice President Richard Cheney, Secretary of Defense Donald Rumsfeld, National Security Advisor Condoleezza Rice, and others on the president's staff believed that Saddam Hussein had been involved in the September 11 attack on the United States.

In 2002 President Bush began to prepare Americans for the idea of sending military forces to Iraq and removing Saddam Hussein from power. This would be a "preemptive" strike, which meant that the United States would attack Iraq in order to prevent Saddam Hussein from attacking first. Otherwise, the president believed, Iraq was sure to strike at the United States.

This tactic was a serious change in foreign policy, because Americans generally thought of themselves as a nation that waged war only in self-defense. President Bush needed to persuade Congress, and the people, to support his plan. In speeches and press conferences, the president and his advisors warned that Iraq had weapons of mass destruction and was developing more powerful weapons.

If Saddam Hussein were left in power in Iraq, the Bush administration said, sooner or later he would use his weapons on other countries. Saddam Hussein might poison water supplies, cause a serious smallpox epidemic, or even launch a nuclear attack. After the September 11, 2001, attacks on New York and Washington, these worst-case scenarios seemed all too possible.

The Bush administration's approach to foreign policy became known as the Bush Doctrine. It was based on the fact that the United States is the most powerful nation in the world. Because the United States was founded on the ideal of freedom for all, it had the responsibility to use its power to promote freedom.

President Bush wanted to lead a coalition of nations to fight terrorism, but it would act alone if necessary. A major goal of the Bush Doctrine was preventing terrorist organizations and countries who aided them from getting and using weapons of mass destruction. The United States should not wait until such weapons were actually used, President Bush argued, but attack *before* they could be used.

In September 2002, a year after al-Qaeda's strikes on the Twin Towers and the Pentagon, President Bush addressed the General Assembly of the United Nations. He urged the UN to pass a resolution demanding that Saddam Hussein allow weapons inspectors into Iraq again, to determine whether Iraq possessed weapons of mass destruction or not. The UN did not act right away, but in October 2002 Congress passed a resolution authorizing President Bush to use force against Iraq. In both the Senate and the House of Representatives this resolution won by a large margin. The next month the United Nations passed a resolution ordering Iraq to disarm or face the consequences.

President Bush's critics, in the U.S. and other countries, were not convinced Saddam Hussein was that dangerous. True, everyone agreed that he was a brutal dictator. He had invaded Kuwait and threatened other neighboring countries, and he had killed and tortured thousands of his own people. Since the end of the first Gulf War in 1991, however, Saddam Hussein seemed to have lost much of his ability to harm other countries. Early in 2003, fearing invasion, he allowed United Nations inspectors back into Iraq. Contrary to what they expected, the inspectors did not find any clear evidence that Iraq still had weapons of mass destruction.

President Bush, however, was sure that the United States could not be safe until Saddam Hussein and his Ba'ath party were overthrown. He also believed that if a democratic government took root in Iraq, it could influence the whole Middle East for the better. That part of the world had suffered under harsh governments, poverty, and warfare for a long time. The president believed it would be a great achievement to turn the troubled region toward freedom, peace, and prosperity.

President Bush tried to persuade the United Nations to cooperate in invading Iraq. But the UN held back, waiting for proof from the inspectors that Saddam Hussein actually possessed weapons of mass destruction. France and Germany, important European allies of the United States, refused outright to join the U.S.'s military coalition.

By the spring of 2003 Britain was the only major U.S. ally willing to help depose Saddam Hussein. But President Bush and his advisors had already decided that the United States would act by itself if it had to. In March U.S. forces began the attack on Baghdad, the capital of Iraq.

Within three weeks Saddam Hussein and his ruling Ba'ath party were deposed, and U.S. troops occupied Baghdad. Although Saddam Hussein's government was toppled, the dictator eluded capture. Still, Iraq had been liberated from its dictator, with the loss of only 135 American lives. The military estimated that about three thousand Iraqi soldiers had been killed. Other news sources reported that several thousand Iraqi civilians had died in the attacks.

Shortly afterward, President Bush celebrated the victory in Iraq with a dramatic gesture. Dressed in a pilot's flight suit, he personally landed a fighter jet on the deck of the *Abraham Lincoln,* an aircraft carrier full of soldiers returning from Iraq. A huge banner behind him proclaimed MISSION ACCOMPLISHED. "Major combat operations in Iraq have ended," announced President Bush.

At first the Americans were welcomed in Iraq as liberators, especially by the Kurds and the Shi'ites. The Kurds, non-Arab Sunni Muslims in northeastern Iraq, and the Shi'ites, a major branch of Islam, were two groups that had been harshly oppressed by Saddam Hussein. The United States announced its plan to gradually withdraw American troops and transfer control of the country to the Iraqi people. A temporary Iraqi government would take over from the American administrator next summer. The U.S. would help Iraq set up a democratic system of government, including fair elections.

But meanwhile, with Saddam Hussein and his brutal dictatorship gone, there was no one to keep order in Iraq except the Americans. Most of the other nations of the world were outraged that the United States had acted alone in launching the war. This feeling prevented them from helping to keep the peace or rebuild Iraq, especially as long as the U.S. was controlling the country.

The American troops were not trained as police, and there weren't enough of them. As a result there was widespread looting in Baghdad and other areas. After twenty years of Saddam Hussein's rule, damage done by the war, and then post-war looting, Iraq was in disarray. The citizens couldn't count on ordinary services like water and electricity, or even public safety. Thieves, kidnappers, and assassins roamed the streets.

On the one hand, the United States had certainly defeated Saddam Hussein. The dictator's older sons, who would have succeeded him, were both killed by U.S. troops in July of 2003. Saddam himself was finally captured at the end of 2003. But more and more people began to ask whether the United States could "win the peace" in Iraq.

Saddam Hussein's Ba'athists continued to fight the American occupation, and anti-American forces from other countries arrived in Iraq to help them. Many Shi'ite Muslims, although they had been sworn enemies of Saddam Hussein's Sunni Muslims, joined the effort to drive Americans out of the country. U.S. soldiers and other American workers, as well as anyone supporting the

Americans, continued to be fired upon and ambushed. By the end of July 2004 over 900 American troops had been killed in Iraq.

The cost of the war in money grew too. At the beginning of the war in Iraq President Bush had said that it would cost the U.S. $74.8 billion. In September 2003 the president announced that he would ask Congress for another $87 billion to keep order in Iraq and rebuild the country. In the spring of 2004 Defense Secretary Donald Rumsfeld told a Senate committee that another $25 billion would be needed for Iraq. It seemed the total cost of the war and reconstruction would actually be nearer to $200 billion.

Meanwhile, early in 2003, a United States congressional commission, known as the 9/11 Commission, began investigating the disaster of September 11, 2001. The idea was that the U.S. needed to understand how the al-Qaeda terrorists had planned and carried out their attacks on New York and Washington. Why hadn't the U.S. prevented the attacks, or at least prevented them from causing so much damage? How could such attacks be prevented in the future?

In the early months of 2004 two former members of

the Bush administration publicly criticized President Bush and his chief advisors. Former Secretary of the Treasury Paul O'Neill, in Ron Suskind's book *The Price of Loyalty,* criticized President Bush for cutting taxes and sending the country deeper into debt. O'Neill also claimed that the Bush administration had planned the war on Iraq even before the September 11 attacks.

Former security advisor Richard Clarke, in his book *Against All Enemies,* accused George W. Bush and his advisors of ignoring clear warnings of a terrorist attack before September 11, 2001. Shortly after Clarke's book came out, the 9/11 Commission issued some disturbing statements. They reported that the government had not protected the United States against a terrorist attack as well as it could have. The Central Intelligence Agency (CIA, which gathers and analyzes information in foreign countries) and the Federal Bureau of Investigation (FBI, the law enforcement arm of the U.S. government) had not shared important information with each other. During 2001 they had missed important hints of the coming attack on September 11.

The 9/11 Commission had also found that the Pentagon had been unprepared for attacks by hijacked airplanes. They also criticized President Bush and his staff for responding to the attacks in a slow and disorganized way.

In April 2004 President and Laura Bush took a much-needed vacation at their ranch in Crawford, Texas. The Bush ranch is a peaceful spread of 1600 acres, planted with native grasses and wildflowers. Here they could hike, fish, swim, and enjoy their family, dogs, and friends in privacy. Even though George W. Bush was still working—talking on the phone, holding meetings, holding conferences with the media—he could be more relaxed on the ranch than in Washington. But toward the end of the month, some especially bad news arrived from Iraq.

The TV news-magazine *60 Minutes II* ran a horrifying story about Abu Ghraib, a prison outside Baghdad. Photographs and eyewitness testimony showed that some American soldiers had badly mistreated their Iraqi prisoners. Americans were deeply shocked and saddened by the news, especially since the mission of the United States was to bring friendship and freedom to Iraq. President Bush's approval rating sank to 46 percent.

Around the world other countries condemned the United States for allowing the abuses of prisoners of war. Many Arab nations, already inclined to think that the United States had waged war on Iraq in order to expand its empire, were especially outraged and furious over the Abu Ghraib scandal. Anti-American terrorist groups used the scandal to recruit more members. More and more, Americans questioned whether the war in Iraq had been worth the cost in lives or money.

CHAPTER 17

ELECTION 2004

MEANWHILE PRESIDENT GEORGE W. BUSH'S FIRST term was nearing its end. The presidential election of 2004 loomed in November. The Democratic primaries early in 2004 had quickly sorted out the candidates, and Senator John F. Kerry of Massachusetts seemed sure to be nominated at the Democratic convention in July.

Senator Kerry accused George W. Bush of increasing the national debt with his massive tax cuts and defense spending. This was the first time in American history that the government had cut taxes while waging a war. John Kerry also blamed President Bush for jobs lost by Americans to low-wage workers in other countries. And he criticized the president for the fact that medical care was so expensive, and that one-fifth of Americans, including millions of children, had no health insurance.

As President Bush's reelection team planned a campaign against Senator Kerry, they thought that Kerry had some serious weaknesses. For many years most American voters had been suspicious of liberal politicians. They connected "liberals" with high taxes and wasteful government spending.

John Kerry, however, had one clear advantage over George W. Bush: The senator was a combat veteran, decorated with several medals for his service during the Vietnam War. During that same war, George W. Bush had only served in the Texas Air National Guard. There was even some question about whether he had completed his duty properly.

Polls showed the voters fairly evenly divided between Bush and Kerry, but it seemed that most Kerry supporters were actually anti-Bush, rather than pro-Kerry. In October 2002 Senator Kerry had voted with the majority of Congress to give the president the power to wage war on Iraq. However, Kerry found himself supported by the voters who thought the war in Iraq had been a mistake from the beginning. And more and more, he was joined by voters who thought the Bush administration had "lost the peace"—mismanaged the occupation of Iraq. So unless feelings about Senator Kerry changed, the election would be decided by voters choosing whether they wanted to stick with President Bush or replace him. George W. Bush's reelection campaign was in trouble.

In many ways President Bush's situation in 2004 was like his father's in the presidential campaign of 1992. At the end of the short and successful Gulf War in 1991, former President George H. W. Bush had been tremendously popular. But when the economy slumped, voters quickly turned against him. They didn't know much about the Democratic candidate, Arkansas Governor Bill Clinton, but they wanted a change.

Fortunately for George W. Bush's reelection campaign in 2004, Laura Bush's popularity remained high, especially with women. While the president's popularity had dropped alarmingly, most women saw his wife as intelligent and sincere. In the spring of 2004 Laura Bush began to campaign actively for her husband's reelection.

The polls tipped a little toward George W. Bush, then a little toward John Kerry. The economy improved and President Bush's approval ratings went up. The situation in Iraq worsened, and the president's approval ratings went down.

As the summer went on, the race for president continued to be very close. The 2004 election was unusual
in that so many voters were paying close attention even
before the Democratic and Republican conventions.
Americans thought the results of this election mattered
much more than they had in 2000. And most of them had
already made up their minds. The polls showed the voters
fairly evenly divided between President Bush and Senator
Kerry, with a small number of voters undecided.

On June 28 the United States occupation turned
over power to a temporary Iraqi government. But there
was still widespread disorder in Iraq. The Ba'athists,
Saddam Hussein's supporters, were fighting to regain
control of the country. Terrorists killed Westerners and
Iraqis with suicide bombs and kidnapped foreigners for
grisly videotaped executions. And criminals continued to
terrorize the citizens. So American troops—140,000 of
them—remained in the country. Even this number was
not enough to keep the peace.

In the United States, George W. Bush had not been
able to bring the country together, as he hoped at the
beginning of his presidency. The goodwill that followed
the attacks of September 11 had long since evaporated.

By the summer of 2004 the United States was even more sharply divided than it had been during the campaign of 2000.

If George Bush lost this election, it seemed, it would be because of his decision to go to war in Iraq. Yet President Bush was convinced he was doing the right thing, even if it cost him the presidency.

Before the Democratic National Convention in July, John Kerry chose Senator John Edwards, a Southerner from North Carolina, as his running mate. During their convention, the Democrats emphasized Senator Kerry's service in the Vietnam War. The Republican National Convention, held in New York City at the beginning of September, focused on President Bush's current role as commander-in-chief of the armed forces. The location of the Republican National Convention and the month it was held reminded voters of the terrorist attacks of September 11, 2001. Many Americans feared another attack and believed that George W. Bush could best defend the country.

During October, President Bush debated John Kerry three times on national TV. Kerry was a more polished speaker than President Bush, and some commentators declared that the senator had "won" the debates. But polls showed that the debates did not change many voters' minds.

Other events in October 2004 made big headlines: Former president Bill Clinton, although recovering from major heart surgery, campaigned for John Kerry. In Iraq it was discovered that 380 tons of explosives had been stolen from a munitions storage facility and were perhaps now being used to attack the American occupying force. And only four days before the election, al-Qaeda leader Osama bin Laden appeared on television for the first time in over a year. Any of these factors *might* affect the election results, but no one could be sure how.

This was the most expensive presidential race ever, and television advertisements made up a large part of the cost. In the last week alone, the total spending for TV ads reached $60 million. But with the Bush and Kerry supporters so evenly divided, the winning side would be the one that actually got its voters to the polls. So legions of Republican and Democratic volunteers went door to door and made phone calls, personally encouraging registered voters to go to the polls.

Both Democrats and Republicans concentrated their efforts in the "swing"—or battleground—states, meaning states where it was unclear whether President Bush or

John Kerry would win. Some of the fiercest battleground states were Florida (27 electoral votes), as in 2000; Pennsylvania (21 electoral votes); and Ohio (20 electoral votes).

This campaign had been long and exhausting, but in the final days George W. Bush seemed more energized than ever. "I'm really having a good time," he told his advisors as they flew from one cheering rally to another.

After the contested election of 2000, both Republicans and Democrats were suspicious that the other party would try to win this election unfairly. President Bush's supporters were afraid the Democrats would register ineligible voters, such as convicted felons or non-citizen immigrants. Senator Kerry's team accused Republicans of trying to prevent low-income African-Americans, who tended to vote Democratic, from going to the polls.

Fortunately, on Election Day—Tuesday, November 2— the biggest problem at the polls turned out to be long lines. Americans showed up to vote in record numbers, about 120 million. This was 60 percent of eligible voters, the highest turnout since 1968. In some places people waited for as long as three hours to cast their votes. Millions were voting for the first time.

At 7:30 Tuesday morning George W. Bush, Laura Bush,

and their daughters arrived at their appointed polling place, the fire station in the tiny town of Crawford, Texas. President Bush then flew to Columbus, Ohio, for one last campaign stop. By Tuesday afternoon he was back at the White House. He would await the election results there with his family.

The large turnout of new voters worried Republicans, because 60 percent of these first-time voters said they supported Senator Kerry. Also, early exit polls (interviews of people who have just voted) on this Election Day seemed to show John Kerry ahead. Some pollsters confidently predicted that Senator Kerry would be elected.

The polls first closed on the East Coast, and the returns began to come in. As the returns from the Midwest and South came in, the Republicans grew steadily more cheerful. President Bush was holding on to almost all the states that he had won in 2000. Furthermore, he was ahead in Florida, the state so bitterly contested in the last election. All over the country, a large number of voters told interviewers that they had chosen the president because of his strong faith and his stance on "moral values"—issues such as abortion and gay marriage. Americans might be worried about the economy and the war in Iraq, but they felt that George W. Bush represented their values better than John Kerry did.

Shortly after midnight two TV networks, Fox News and NBC, predicted that George W. Bush had won Ohio. That would give him 274 electoral votes, four more than he needed to win. The Bush campaign expected John Kerry to call the White House soon to officially acknowledge that President Bush had won the election. At the Ronald Reagan Building near the White House, the Republican election-night party prepared to welcome President Bush as the victor.

But by 2:45 A.M., Senator Kerry had still not conceded. At the Democratic election-night party in Boston, vice-presidential nominee John Edwards announced that the Democrats would wait for the final returns in Ohio. If Ohio went to Senator Kerry after all, the Democrats could still win.

However, at 11:00 A.M. on Wednesday, November 3, George W. Bush finally received a call from John Kerry. "Congratulations, Mr. President," said the senator from Massachusetts. To the relief of most Americans, there would not be a repeat of the contested election of 2000.

At 3:00 P.M., President Bush appeared at the Ronald

Reagan Building to celebrate his victory. As he spoke to the nation, his overjoyed supporters kept interrupting with thunderous applause. "America has spoken," said George W. Bush, "and I'm humbled by the trust and the confidence of my fellow citizens."

In this election, President Bush had won a more solid victory than in 2000. He had won the popular vote— 51 percent of it—as well as the electoral vote. Across the country, Republicans had gained seats in the House and Senate, so President Bush could count on the support of Congress in his second term.

However, the problems that President Bush and the country faced at the end of 2004 were graver than in 2000. The bloody and costly war in Iraq dragged on. Furthermore, that war was distracting the United States from dealing with other serious problems. Nations unfriendly to the U.S., such as North Korea, were producing nuclear weapons. World oil supplies, on which the modern way of life depended, were dwindling fast. At home, the country needed to improve education, grow the economy, provide health insurance for all Americans, and make the country secure against terrorist attacks.

Still, President Bush was eager to get to work on his

goals for his second term. As he told a press conference two days after the election, he intended to reform Social Security, simplify the tax laws, and use foreign policy to win the War on Terror. And he believed he could accomplish all this: "I've got the will of the people at my back."

CHAPTER 18
"ENDING TYRANNY IN OUR WORLD"

BEFORE THE BEGINNING OF HIS SECOND TERM, President Bush announced some changes in his administration. The biggest change was a new secretary of state, replacing Colin Powell. Powell had planned on serving only one term, but he also felt that the president's team did not work together very well. Especially, he felt that Vice President Cheney and Secretary of Defense Rumsfeld had too much influence in U.S. relations with other countries. The area of foreign relations was the responsibility of the State Department, not the Department of Defense.

George Bush decided to replace Powell with his national security advisor, Condoleezza Rice. He had known "Condi," as he called her, for many years, and he respected her keen intellect, her knowledge of international politics, and her skill in handling people. George and Condi had a close, trusting working relationship, and he often invited her for dinner with him and Laura at the White House.

Many of the president's advisors wished he would replace Secretary of Defense Donald Rumsfeld as well. Rumsfeld was held responsible for many of the mistakes in the increasingly unpopular Iraq War. But Bush felt it was unfair to blame Rumsfeld for the problems in Iraq, and Vice President Cheney was a firm backer of Rumsfeld.

Bush deeply valued Cheney's opinion. Dick Cheney was widely acknowledged to be the most powerful vice president in the history of the United States. He had much more influence on President George W. Bush than, for instance, Vice President George H. W. Bush had had on President Ronald Reagan. Cheney believed that the United States, as the world's only superpower, could pursue its goals without consulting its allies. He also believed that negotiating with hostile nations, such as North Korea, was a waste of time, and that they would respond only to force or to threats of force.

However, George Bush's choice of Condoleezza Rice for secretary of state signaled that he intended to steer foreign policy in a different direction. Rice believed in using diplomacy whenever possible, even with enemies, and she also believed in working closely with friendly nations. President Bush listened to Rice carefully when she told him that the United States had "repair work to do with the allies."

On January 20, 2005, George W. Bush delivered the inauguration speech for his second term. He was excited and hopeful about what he could accomplish, and he wanted his speech to sweep the American people along with him. He set a high goal for the United States and its allies: "ending tyranny in our world." Before the inauguration, Secretary of State Rice had questioned whether this goal was too big and too vague. But Bush wanted to remind the nation, and the rest of the world, that the United States of America stood for freedom.

President Bush hoped that the coming election in Iraq would move that country toward becoming a peaceful democracy. It was certainly a milestone for the Iraqi people: their first election since the dictator Saddam Hussein had been toppled in 2003. If all went well, the citizens of Iraq would choose their own leaders to make the transition between U.S. control of the country and independence for Iraq.

As George Bush knew, it was a complicated situation. The three main groups in Iraq, the Shi'ites, the Ba'athist Sunnis, and the Kurds, hated and distrusted one another. The Ba'athists threatened to boycott the election and punish any Iraqis who did turn out to vote.

In some areas voter turnout was low among Sunnis, in response to bombings and other violence by Ba'athists before the election. And the Ba'athists did carry out attacks on some polling places. However, in spite of this, the election seemed to go fairly well. Bush felt it was a triumph for democracy in Iraq.

The hopeful news from Iraq convinced President Bush that the warring factions would now form a new government and stop fighting with one another. When U.S. troops were no longer needed to keep order, he could withdraw them with a clear conscience. Seeing this outcome in the near future, Bush assumed that the United States could now focus on problems at home. In his State of the Union address, he described his ambitious domestic plans for the next four years.

George Bush had already outlined what he wanted to do in his 2004 campaign speeches the previous year: revise the United States's complicated and hated income tax code, liberalize immigration laws, and reform the Social Security Administration. The voters had reelected him, as well as electing a majority of Republicans to both the House of Representatives and the Senate. So Bush believed that the people of the United States were solidly behind his plans. The president was especially concerned about the weaknesses of the Social Security system, and overhauling it was first on his list.

Ever since 1935, this government program had sent payments to Americans who were considered too old to have to support themselves. Before Social Security, half the elderly people in the United States, unemployed or unable to work, and without sufficient savings, had lived in poverty. The program was gradually expanded to include other groups, such as the disabled and the spouses and dependent children of retirees.

The trouble was, the money for Social Security payments came out of the earnings of present-day workers. In 1950 the average life expectancy in the United States was about sixty-eight. So if a worker retired at age sixty-five, he or she would probably need only a few years' worth of Social Security payments. But by 2002, life expectancy had risen to about seventy-seven, and it was predicted to keep on rising.

It was believed that if more and more Americans continued to live longer and longer, there would not be enough workers to pay for the needs of all the elderly retirees.

In the spring of 2005 President Bush toured the country, speaking to groups and on television to generate support for reform. He declared that unless the system was changed, Social Security would run out of funds by the year 2042. But he didn't want to get too specific about how the problem could be solved. He knew that the steps necessary for reforming Social Security, such as raising the retirement age and increasing Social Security deductions from workers' paychecks, would be very unpopular. Instead he talked about his idea to allow Americans to invest a portion of their Social Security funds in the stock market.

But the more President Bush talked about reforming Social Security, the more uneasy Americans became. Millions of older Americans depended on their Social Security checks to pay for basic needs like food and rent, and it made them nervous to even hear talk of changing the system. There was a good reason why politicians called Social Security the "third rail" of American politics. This expression compares the subject of Social Security to the third rail in a railway track, the rail that carries a powerful and dangerous electric charge. If you even touch it, you'll be electrocuted.

"I did more than touch the third rail," Bush admitted later in his memoir *Decision Points*. "I hugged it." Democrats pounced on the opportunity to accuse President Bush of trying to destroy Social Security. The Republicans in Congress, fearing the voters' wrath in the coming elections of 2006, refused to go along with Bush's plan. So Social Security reform, one of his major initiatives for the next four years, had already failed.

Another important goal George W. Bush had in mind for his second term was to reform the immigration system. About eleven million immigrants, most of them from Mexico, were living in the United States without visas, work permits, or any kind of official and legal permission. Some Republicans thought the solution was to send all eleven million undocumented immigrants back to the countries they came from.

But Bush knew that was impossible. Besides, he thought the present immigration system was unfair to employers in agriculture, the service industry, and other low-skill jobs, who could be punished for hiring the workers they needed. It was also unfair to the undocumented immigrant workers. Because they were afraid of being arrested and deported if they complained to the police, they could be underpaid and made to work under unsafe conditions.

Bush proposed a guest worker plan, so that foreign laborers could temporarily work in the United States without fear of being arrested and deported. He also wanted to give some undocumented immigrants a gradual path to citizenship. At the same time, he promised to make the borders of the United States, especially the border with Mexico, more secure, so that fewer immigrants without official permission could enter.

President Bush felt that immigration reform was the right thing to do. Besides, it would win friends for the Republican Party among the growing numbers of Latino voters. But the Republican leadership in Congress refused to cooperate. They were concerned that undocumented immigrants, willing to work for less, took jobs away from U.S. citizens.

The Republicans also believed that such immigrants strained the health care system by receiving free medical treatment, and strained the educational system by sending their children to U.S. schools. There was only one action on immigration they wanted: to secure the border with Mexico so tightly that no more immigrants could enter illegally.

During the spring of 2005, while President Bush waited for Iraq to form a new government, he turned his attention to other countries. He wanted to follow up on his second inaugural speech, in which he had vowed to support democracy and end tyranny around the world. He was concerned about Russia, a very important country in the world community, where human rights were narrowing rather than widening. In the last few years, President Vladimir Putin had clamped down on the media in Russia, punished wealthy businessmen who opposed him, and changed the laws so that governors of regions in the Russian Federation were appointed by him rather than elected by the people.

Bush believed in "personal diplomacy," improving relations between the United States and other countries by making friends with the foreign leaders. For instance, he considered Tony Blair, prime minister of Great Britain, a close friend. Under Blair, Britain was one of the few countries that had supported the United States in invading Iraq in 2003.

In contrast, Russia under Vladimir Putin had come out strongly against the U.S. invasion of Iraq. Even so, George Bush felt he had a genuine friendship with the Russian president, whom he called by his first name, Vladimir. He had welcomed Putin and his wife to the Bush ranch in Crawford as well as to the White House.

But Vice President Cheney and Secretary of State Rice, although they disagreed on many matters, both distrusted Putin. He had been an officer in the KGB, the ruthless secret police of the former Soviet Union. Furthermore, Putin clearly resented the outcome of the Cold War, which had ended with the disbanding of the Soviet Union. He was discontented that instead of two superpowers in the world, the United States and the Soviet Union, there was now only one superpower, the United States.

There was no doubt that Bush's and Putin's political views were far apart. When they met in Slovakia in February 2005, Bush tried to persuade Putin to loosen his control of the newspapers and TV stations in Russia. Putin brushed away the idea, accusing Bush of controlling what the American media said about him.

In May 2005 President Bush traveled to Moscow to meet with the Russian president again. During the visit, Putin compared his own dog, a large black Labrador retriever, to the Bushes' little Scottish terrier, Barney. "Bigger, tougher, stronger, faster, meaner than Barney," said Putin jokingly (or maybe not so jokingly). Putin was displeased when President Bush flew on from Moscow to Georgia, a country that Putin wanted to keep under Russian control.

In Tbilisi, Georgia, President Bush spoke to a crowd of two hundred thousand chanting, "Bushi, Bushi." But as Bush praised the Georgians for their struggle toward democracy and independence, a man in the crowd threw a live grenade toward him. (Later it would come out that the would-be assassin hated the influence of Western countries, including the United States, on Georgia.) Fortunately, the grenade failed to explode.

Bush's personal diplomacy worked with Tony Blair of Great Britain, and it might work with Vladimir Putin of Russia, but he could not use this approach with Iran or North Korea. The United States did not even have direct diplomatic relations with these countries. Iran had considered the United States an enemy since the revolution of 1979, when the country became an Islamic republic. North Korea and the United States had been enemies since the Korean War in the 1950s. The Kim family had ruled North Korea as a military dictatorship, cut off from the rest of the world, for many years.

It was especially worrisome to George Bush and his team that Iran and North Korea were both working to develop nuclear weapons. Secretary of State Rice believed that the best way to persuade these countries to halt their nuclear programs was by "indirect" diplomacy. So the United States stepped aside to let its European allies Britain, Germany, and France try to persuade Iran to give up its nuclear enrichment program. With North Korea, the United States was assisted by China, Japan, Russia, and South Korea in six-party talks. By September 2005, North Korea seemed to be coming around to an agreement.

Meanwhile, President Bush's hopes for a peaceful democracy in Iraq were fading. The three factions of the temporary government had finally managed to elect a prime minister, Nouri al-Maliki, but they could not agree on a new constitution. The violence in Iraq was actually worse than the year before. More Iraqi civilians were killed, and more U.S. and allied troops died. Back in the United States, the issue of mistreatment of prisoners, including those held at Guantánamo, the U.S. military prison in Cuba, came up again. Bush's old rival John McCain proposed a Senate bill to ban the torture of political prisoners, those imprisoned for opposing or criticizing the government. McCain was a loyal Republican, and he backed the War on Terror, but he was against what the Bush administration called "enhanced interrogation." A fighter pilot during the Vietnam War, McCain himself had been tortured as a prisoner in North Vietnam. "What we are is a nation that upholds values and standards of behavior and treatment of all people," he said, "no matter how evil or bad they are."

That summer George Bush flew to his Texas ranch for the month of August. With the Iraq War going so badly, the media criticized Bush for taking a "working vacation." But in George Bush's opinion, it wasn't much of a vacation. "We had just moved the West Wing twelve hundred miles farther west." The president continued to study daily updates on the state of the nation and the world, hold meetings, take trips, and talk with his advisors, especially to discuss Iraq.

Playing golf was one of Bush's favorite ways to relax, but he had given up the sport in 2003. He thought it would look heartless for him to be swinging clubs on a golf course while American soldiers were dying in Iraq.

On his ranch, he relieved the stress of the presidency by biking over mountain trails, or cutting brush in one-hundred-degree heat.

Polls showed that only 38 percent of Americans approved of the way President Bush was conducting the war. Most Americans now felt it had been a mistake to invade Iraq in the first place. George Bush still believed that the United States had done the right thing in bringing down Saddam Hussein. But he was deeply shaken by the ongoing sacrifice of so many American servicemen and servicewomen and their families.

George W. Bush had begun his second term as president in high spirits, but the first half of 2005 had not gone well. And worse was to come. Toward the end of August, when Bush was still at the ranch, he was informed of a Category 1 hurricane named Katrina

CHAPTER 19
THE WORST NATURAL DISASTER

EVERY YEAR, FROM THE BEGINNING OF THE SUMMER to the end of autumn, powerful spiral wind systems form in the North Atlantic Ocean. At wind speeds of thirty-eight to sixty-three miles per hour, they are termed tropical storms. At sixty-four miles per hour, a storm becomes a Category 1 hurricane. Hurricane Betsy, which barreled down on New Orleans in 1965, had been a Category 5, with wind speeds of 155 miles per hour. Betsy had killed dozens of people and done over a billion dollars' worth of damage.

Forty years later, late in August 2005, Tropical Storm Katrina formed over the Bahamas, a chain of islands southeast of Florida. The U.S. National Weather Service warned that the storm was growing and headed for southern Florida. When Katrina swept across southern Florida on August 25, it was "only" a Category 1 hurricane. Still, millions of people in Florida lost electrical power, and several people were killed. George's brother Jeb, the governor of Florida, declared a state of emergency.

Katrina headed west into the Gulf of Mexico. Feeding on the warm water, the hurricane kept growing. By Saturday, August 27, it filled the gulf. The National Hurricane Center had thought at first that the hurricane would swerve northeast over the Florida Panhandle, but now they predicted it would swing north instead and hit the coasts of Louisiana and Mississippi.

By Sunday, August 28, Katrina was a Category 5 hurricane, with wind speeds over 175 miles per hour. It was one of the three most violent hurricanes ever recorded in the United States. And New Orleans, Louisiana, was in its path.

Much of New Orleans, a city of almost half a million people on the Mississippi River delta, was below sea level. New Orleans was protected by levees, or raised embankments, and floodwalls of steel-reinforced concrete along the canals, but hurricanes still caused flooding from time to time. Older residents of New Orleans remembered Hurricane Betsy in 1965, when people had drowned in their attics, trying to escape the rising waters. Every year at hurricane season, they wondered if this would be the year of the dreaded "Big One," a monster storm even worse than Betsy.

At the Bush ranch in Texas, President Bush received bulletins about Katrina's progress. The National Hurricane Center informed him on Sunday that they expected Katrina to cause a storm surge, or flooding above normal tide levels. The levees protecting New Orleans would overflow—how badly, they couldn't say. A powerful storm surge could fill the whole bowl-shaped city with water.

Governor Kathleen Blanco had already declared a state of emergency for Louisiana on Friday, August 26. She advised everyone living in the path of Katrina to leave their homes for a safe area. Ray Nagin, the mayor of New Orleans, also urged his people to evacuate the city. Thousands of cars choked the highways out of New Orleans, as many residents fled the oncoming hurricane.

But a third of the people of New Orleans had no cars, and most of those people did not have the money to pay for transportation. As Senator Barack Obama noted later, they couldn't just "load up their SUV, put one hundred dollars' worth of gas in there, put [in] some sparkling water, and drive off to a hotel and check in with a credit card."

On Sunday, August 28, Mayor Nagin finally *ordered* all residents to leave the city. But there was no plan for their evacuation. By this time, it was too late for tens of thousands of people to get out. Many thousands of them sought refuge in the Superdome, the city's main emergency shelter, although it was prepared with food, cots, and other supplies and equipment for only eight hundred people.

Early on Monday morning, August 29, Hurricane Katrina slammed into the coast of Louisiana. Although its wind speeds had slowed somewhat, they were still up to 145 miles per hour. Between the wind and heavy rain, there was a massive storm surge. The levees around the city overflowed—and then they broke down. The city began to flood.

President Bush was informed that there was some flooding in New Orleans, but he believed that the city of New Orleans, the state of Louisiana, and the Federal Emergency Management Agency (FEMA) would be able to handle the crisis. He left his ranch in Texas for a scheduled trip to California. It was not until Tuesday, August 30, that the president learned how hard New Orleans had been hit. "This was the Big One," Michael D. Brown, the head of FEMA, told the president. President Bush cut his California trip short and headed back to Washington, D.C. He considered landing in the disaster zone to show sympathy for the victims of Katrina but decided that would not be helpful. Any appearance of the president of the United States is a major undertaking, for the hosts as well as the president's team. During this emergency, George Bush didn't want the police in New Orleans or the National Guard of Louisiana to have to worry about his security.

However, Bush told Air Force One to fly over New Orleans so that he could see what was happening for himself. Although he had been told that 80 percent of New Orleans was flooded, he was shocked at the sight below him. It looked more like a lake than a city.

Whole neighborhoods were under water, with only a rooftop or a floating car here and there. Bridges had been washed away, and the outer covering of the huge Superdome had been peeled off by the high winds. All along the coasts of Alabama, Mississippi, and Louisiana, Hurricane Katrina had flattened town after town and knocked whole forests down like matchsticks.

Americans watching the disaster unfold on TV news saw the same aerial scenes of destruction, but they also saw horrific pictures from ground level. Dead bodies, human as well as animal, floated in the New Orleans canals. Families clung to their rooftops amid rising waters. Fleets of empty New Orleans city buses, which could have been used earlier to carry the residents out of harm's way, sat in flooded parking lots.

Even after the waters stopped rising, the city remained flooded for several days. New Orleans depends on a system of pumps to keep water outside the levees, and the pumps had failed. The U.S. Coast Guard worked around the clock with boats and helicopters to rescue stranded people.

At the New Orleans Superdome, more than twenty thousand people, including helpless residents from nursing homes and families with babies, huddled under the leaking roof. The electricity failed, leaving them without lights or air conditioning. The sewage system also failed.

By Wednesday morning, August 31, supplies had run out in the shelters. Emergency workers raided nearby stores for food and water to bring back to the refugees. It was not until Friday, September 2, that the National Guard arrived in New Orleans. They distributed supplies and began transporting hurricane victims from the dark, filthy, sweltering hot Superdome. Many of them were taken to the Astrodome in Houston, Texas.

Aside from the Coast Guard, the response to Katrina was slow and confused. It wasn't clear who was in charge in New Orleans—Ray Nagin, the mayor? Kathleen Blanco, the governor of Louisiana? Michael D. Brown, director of FEMA? The city was in chaos, and the New Orleans Police Department was not able to keep order.

Some of Bush's team wanted U.S. troops sent in, but Secretary of Defense Rumsfeld felt that would look too much like a military takeover. The National Guard from several states was called in. Finally President Bush ordered federal troops (without weapons) to New Orleans to serve as humanitarian workers.

Hurricane Katrina turned out to be the costliest natural disaster in U.S. history, with property damage alone amounting to more than $100 billion. Along the Gulf Coast, oil platforms and refineries were destroyed or damaged, cutting off supplies of crude oil, gasoline, and natural gas to the rest of the country. Over a million acres of commercial forest in Mississippi were smashed flat. Highways and bridges could not be used, and the normally vast flow of exports through the Port of New Orleans and other Gulf Coast ports was interrupted.

More than 1,800 people died as a result of the hurricane and flooding. One million Americans were uprooted from their homes. Hundreds of thousands of people lost their jobs, and many of them had to leave the area for good.

There were many reasons why Hurricane Katrina was such a disaster:

- It was one of the most intense hurricanes ever to make landfall in the United States.
- A great part of the wetlands that once protected Louisiana, acting as sponges to sop up floodwaters, had been degraded or destroyed by human activity, including oil extraction, logging, and some flood control methods.
- The levee system to protect New Orleans from flooding, designed by the U.S. Army Corps of Engineers after Congress passed the Flood Control Act of 1965, was flawed. Furthermore, the system had not been completed or even well maintained by the responsible federal, state, and city agencies.
- Much of New Orleans, especially the densely

populated poorer sections, stood on land below sea level.

• The lower-income people of New Orleans were not able to leave the city before the hurricane struck.

• The hurricane knocked down telephone lines and cell towers, making it hard to coordinate relief efforts.

• There was confusion among the authorities in the city of New Orleans, the state of Louisiana, and the U.S. government about who was in charge of responding to the disaster. And none of these agencies had made adequate preparations.

Most of these factors were not President Bush's fault, but Katrina was also a costly disaster for his public image. Along with all the photos of destruction and suffering in New Orleans, Americans saw pictures of George Bush staring out the window of Air Force One, surveying the devastation from a distance. Viewers got the mistaken impression that President Bush didn't care about the desperate people below.

President Bush was also blamed for having appointed Michael D. Brown, nicknamed "Brownie," as director of the Federal Emergency Management Agency. In a TV appearance on September 2, Bush said, "Brownie, you're doing a heck of a job." He meant to appear upbeat and encouraging, but it only made him seem out of touch in the middle of a national tragedy.

The people who suffered the most from Hurricane Katrina were those who had few resources to begin with, and a large proportion of the victims were African-American. During a TV fund-raiser for Katrina victims, Kanye West, a popular rapper, said, "George Bush doesn't care about black people." George told Laura that this was the worst moment of his presidency. He felt that this criticism was deeply untrue and unfair.

George Bush wrote later, in his memoir *Decision Points,* that he should have urged the mayor of New Orleans and the governor of Louisiana to evacuate the city earlier. He should have come straight back to Washington from California as soon as he learned about the flooding. Also, he felt he should have overruled Secretary of Defense Rumsfeld and sent U.S. troops into New Orleans sooner.

Bush also wished he had expressed his sympathy and concern for the hurricane victims right away. He had *felt* sympathy and concern, but he had not communicated

199

his feelings to the nation. In contrast, after the attacks of September 11, 2001, Americans had seen him as a strong, concerned leader. Because of his response to that disaster, his popularity had soared.

President Bush made sure that the areas hit by Katrina received federal funds, amounting to $126 billion, for disaster relief and reconstruction. He and Laura visited the disaster locations many times to sympathize with and encourage the victims. But in the opinion of most Americans, he had failed to lead the response to Hurricane Katrina. His popularity never recovered.

The first year of George W. Bush's second term as president had been full of disappointments and disasters: Hurricane Katrina, the ongoing Iraq War, the failures of Social Security reform and immigration reform. In addition, all the painstaking diplomacy with North Korea to end its nuclear weapons program had gone nowhere, and those talks were dropped.

But President Bush was glad that at least he had filled two vacancies on the Supreme Court with new conservative justices. These were important appointments, since the Supreme Court has the power to decide momentous issues for the whole nation. For instance, in 2001 it was the Supreme Court that ruled that George W. Bush, rather than Al Gore, would become the forty-third president of the United States.

The vacancies on the court in 2005 were left by Justice Sandra Day O'Connor, who announced her retirement in July, and Chief Justice William Rehnquist, who died in September. Bush nominated John Roberts, circuit judge in the District of Columbia, as the new chief justice. Roberts was quickly confirmed by the Senate.

Bush had more trouble filling the second vacancy. He leaned toward picking a woman, and at first he chose Harriet Miers, his White House counsel. But as soon as President Bush announced his choice, conservative Republicans in Congress announced that they would reject Miers. Bush was angry that his own party members in Congress did not support his choice, but then people of many different political views criticized Miers as not qualified to serve on the Supreme Court. Before the confirmation hearings in the Senate could begin, she asked President Bush to withdraw her nomination.

In place of Harriet Miers he proposed Samuel Alito, the federal appeals court judge in New Jersey. Alito was strongly and openly conservative in his politics, and Bush knew that right-wing Republicans would approve of him. On the other hand, he knew that the Democrats in the Senate would fight the nomination. They did question Alito in an unfriendly way, but by early 2006, Alito was also confirmed.

Meanwhile, Senator John McCain was making good progress with the Detainee Treatment Act, his proposed law to ban the torture of prisoners suspected of terrorism. McCain was supported by many retired generals and admirals, including Colin Powell. In October the Senate overwhelmingly approved the Detainee Treatment Act.

Bush considered vetoing the bill, but Secretary of State Rice advised him not to. She was well aware that accusations of torture were harming the reputation of the United States around the world. And more damaging information had just come out. The media revealed that the Central Intelligence Agency (CIA) was holding suspects for questioning in "black sites" or secret prisons in eastern Europe.

The Detainee Treatment Act became law in December 2005. But Vice President Cheney and his staff had worked behind the scenes to amend it, and the final bill restricted CIA interrogators much less than Senator McCain had intended. The new law said only that interrogation techniques should not be "cruel and unusual" or "shock the conscience." And when President Bush signed the bill into law, he also issued a statement that he reserved the right to interpret the law. If the terms of the Detainee Treatment Act came into conflict with the president's duty of "protecting the American people from further terrorist attacks," he would decide which was more important.

CHAPTER 20
THE DECIDER

SOME IN PRESIDENT BUSH'S INNER CIRCLE THOUGHT
that he should have picked a new vice president for his second term. Unlike most politicians, Vice President Cheney did not care what other people thought of him, and he made no effort to improve his public image. His political enemies often accused him of pushing the younger, less experienced George Bush to launch the Iraq War in 2003, and to allow mistreatment of military prisoners. George W. Bush was not as easily pushed around as some people imagined, but he had deep respect for Cheney, and he never considered replacing him as vice president.

At the beginning of 2006 the war in Iraq was going from bad to worse. Bush had counted on the elections in 2005 to move Iraq toward a peaceful democracy. But more than a year later, the Shi'ites, the Sunnis, and the Kurds in the Iraqi parliament had not been able to cooperate and form a new government.

Then al-Qaeda, the terrorist organization that was responsible for the attacks on the United States in 2001, bombed the Golden Mosque, a precious holy site to all Shi'ite Muslims in Samarra. In Baghdad, the capital of Iraq, Sunnis and Shi'ites fought in the streets. Hundreds of Iraqis were killed, and the violence threatened to boil over into civil war.

Back in the United States there was less and less support for U.S. intervention in Iraq. In 2003 Vice President Cheney had told the American public to expect the war to cost the United States $100 billion. But as of 2006 Congress had appropriated more than three times that much for the Iraq War, more than 2,000 American troops had died there, and no end was in sight.

U.S. citizens who had opposed the war continued to hold protest marches and demonstrations. In addition some conservatives who had formerly backed the war changed their minds. And a report by the heads of U.S. intelligence groups concluded that the Iraq War had actually made Islamic terrorism worse and increased the threat of terrorism.

Many people were convinced that Secretary of Defense Donald Rumsfeld had mishandled the Iraq War from the beginning. In Congress, within President Bush's team of advisors, and among retired generals, a chorus of voices rose urging the president to fire Rumsfeld. But George Bush would not give in.

In April the president appeared in the Rose Garden of the White House to speak to reporters. "I'm the decider and I decide what is best," he said. "And what's best is for Don Rumsfeld to remain as the secretary of defense." That statement earned President Bush the nickname "the Decider," which would follow him even after he left the presidency. But Bush didn't mind if people laughed at his choice of words.

What did trouble George Bush, deeply, was the situation in Iraq. He had launched the war with the hope that the United States could turn Iraq into a peaceful democracy, an example to the rest of the Middle East. But three years later that goal seemed nowhere near. And U.S. troops were still dying in Iraq.

George met with hundreds of American families whose loved ones had died in the Iraq War. He also visited hundreds of soldiers who had been badly wounded. Some of the military members and their families were proud of their service and supported the president's policy in Iraq. Some of them blamed him for their suffering—one mother told Bush he was "as big a terrorist as Osama bin Laden." Either way, these meetings were painful, but they were part of the president's job, as commander-in-chief of the armed forces of the United States.

The bad news kept coming from Iraq: bombings, assassinations, Iraqis killing other Iraqis, Iraqis killing Americans, and even one incident in which American troops killed Iraqi civilians. The city of Baghdad was so dangerous for U.S. civilian officials that they had to stay inside the fortlike Green Zone. The president's advisors worried that the strain would be too much for Bush, although he was determined not to show his discouragement in public.

But Laura Bush knew how worried her husband was. To help relieve his stress, she often invited George's brother Marvin to the White House. With his younger brother, the president of the United States could watch sports on television and relax for a while, as if they were just two ordinary fans.

Although George Bush would not let anyone tell him what to do about Iraq, he was willing to listen to Secretary of State Condoleezza Rice on other issues. She wanted him to close the secret "black site" prisons where the CIA had been holding terror suspects for questioning. Rice, as well as many others, believed that by this time not much information was to be gained from such suspects. In any case, it was not worth the stain on the country's reputation. Vice President Cheney vigorously disagreed.

On September 6 President Bush announced that the secret prisons in eastern Europe were being closed. The few prisoners left in them would be sent to Guantánamo. However, Bush also defended the use of harsh interrogation for getting information from terrorists. Such information, he said, had "saved innocent lives by helping us stop new attacks here in the United States and around the world."

At the beginning of his second term in 2005, President Bush had made a major point that the United States stood for freedom. He believed sincerely that if people had the chance to vote in free and fair elections, they would make the right choices. In January 2006 that belief was tested by Palestinian elections, the first in ten years.

The Palestinian problem in Israel was also a problem

for the United States. Israel was the strongest ally of the United States in the Middle East. But ever since the founding of Israel in 1948, there had been conflicts between the Palestinian Arabs already living in the country and the Jews from all over the world who considered Israel to be their ancient and rightful homeland. Most of the Arab countries of the Middle East refused to recognize Israel as a sovereign state.

Like many presidents before him, George W. Bush was eager to help resolve the Palestine-Israel problem. He strongly supported Israel, but he also thought that the Palestinians had a right to their own separate nation. He hoped the elections in 2006 would give power to Palestinian leaders who were willing to work out a peaceful solution with the Israelis. But, instead, the winner of that election was the Hamas party. Hamas had a history of violence, and it denied that Israel had a right to exist. Discouraged, the Bush administration cut off aid to the Palestinians.

In another part of the world, North Korea continued to be a major concern to the United States. The dictator of North Korea, Kim Jong Il, was still working to develop a nuclear weapon. It was frightening to imagine North Korea using such a weapon against South Korea or other nearby countries. Just as frightening, North Korea might sell nuclear weapons to terrorists such as al-Qaeda.

Since the United States did not have diplomatic relations with North Korea, President Bush asked the Chinese government for help. China did warn Kim Jong Il to halt work on his nuclear program, but he ignored the warnings. In October, North Korea went ahead and tested a nuclear weapon. The world community of nations was horrified, and the United Nations Security Council, including China, punished North Korea with sanctions. But still North Korea did not give up its nuclear program.

Back in the United States the midterm elections for the House of Representatives and the Senate were coming up in November 2006. Republican senators and congressmen worried that President Bush's low approval ratings would rub off on them. In 2001 Bush's approval rating with American voters had been 90 percent, the highest recorded for any president. But by 2006 his approval rating had sunk to 38 percent, one of the lowest ever.

Most Republican candidates did not ask the president to stand beside them on their campaign platforms, as Bush's low approval ratings could affect their ability to get elected. But it was no use—in November, Republicans lost across the country. In Congress, they lost control of both the House and the Senate. They lost the races for governor in many states. As President Bush admitted at a press conference in the East Room of the White House, "It was a thumpin'."

Even before the elections, George Bush had come to the conclusion that it would be best, after all, for Secretary of Defense Donald Rumsfeld to step down. He decided to replace Rumsfeld with Robert Gates, who had been CIA director under President George H. W. Bush. Vice President Cheney disagreed with this decision, calling Rumsfeld "the finest secretary of defense this nation has ever had." But others on the president's team and in the military believed that Rumsfeld had mishandled the Iraq War, and that his unpopularity with a large number of Americans was hurting the Bush administration. They were glad to see Rumsfeld go.

As for the Iraq War, President Bush had formed a bold plan to turn the war around. Instead of withdrawing American forces from Iraq, as most Americans wanted him to do, he decided to send a sudden surge in the number of troops. The president explained his decision before TV cameras on January 10, 2007. He believed that sending twenty thousand more U.S. soldiers to Iraq could quickly halt the violence. Then the battling factions would have the chance to resolve their differences politically, rather than with guns and bombs.

Vice President Cheney approved of the surge, but many others in the Bush administration, including Secretary of State Condoleezza Rice, disagreed with the president. So did the Joint Chiefs of Staff of the United States military. Even the prime minister of Iraq, Nouri al-Maliki, did not want the surge. All the Democrats in Congress, as well as many Republicans, thought Bush was making a terrible mistake. In the spring Congress passed a bill that demanded a deadline for withdrawing U.S. troops from Iraq, but the president refused to sign it.

"It was a hard and lonely decision, and it was one of his bravest moments in office," Laura Bush wrote later. However, she did not let George feel sorry for himself. It had been his own choice, she reminded him, to run for president.

At this time Bush found comfort in thinking about other presidents who had made difficult and unpopular decisions. He had a bust of Abraham Lincoln in his office, and he felt close to this president who had agonized over the Civil War. "I am no Lincoln," he told his aides, "but I am in the same boat."

There were almost two years left in George W. Bush's second term, but already the presidential candidates for the 2008 elections had begun their campaigns. Senator Hillary Clinton of New York and Senator Barack Obama of Illinois, the main Democratic contenders, both criticized President Bush mercilessly. Clinton said Bush's management of the Iraq War had been all wrong, while Obama said it was a "dumb war" to begin with. Worse, the Republican candidates seemed to be trying to outdo one another in attacking President Bush. Senator John McCain described Bush's conduct of the Iraq War as "a train wreck."

But President Bush cared more about halting the slide into civil war than about making popular choices. At the end of 2007 the surge seemed to be working. Iraq was calmer. The number of American soldiers dying there was decreasing.

During 2007 there were some warning signs of another type of disaster looming. "But very few saw it at the time, including me," Bush wrote later. Through the first six years of Bush's presidency, the U.S. economy had grown steadily.

Amid all the other emergencies and ongoing problems, George Bush could console himself that the economy, at least, was strong.

The economy had begun to lag in 2006, but many financial experts thought it was just a temporary slowdown. But at the beginning of 2008 Secretary of the Treasury Henry Paulson informed President Bush that the U.S. economy was in serious trouble. Job growth was slowing almost to a halt. The economic growth had been fueled by the wildly upbeat housing market, or "bubble." And the bubble had burst.

The price of houses had been rising ever since 1998, convincing many people that buying a house was a surefire investment. Thinking that they could always sell a house for more money than they'd paid, they took out home mortgages that they couldn't afford. Also, speculators bought houses only to "flip" them, or resell to make a quick profit. When the price of houses fell sharply in 2007, millions of Americans were stuck with real estate that was worth less than what they had paid for it.

The market for new houses collapsed. Hundreds of thousands of homeowners, unable to make their mortgage payments, lost their homes to foreclosure. During 2008 the unemployment rate climbed as more and more workers in the construction industry lost their jobs. And the damage from the burst housing bubble spread through the whole U.S. economy, in a ripple effect.

Furthermore, Americans in general had taken on a great deal of debt besides mortgages in the last ten years or so. Now they began to pay down the debt instead of spending on credit. Throughout the economy, businesses shrank, more employees lost their jobs, and people had even less money to spend.

Secretary Paulson recommended stimulating the economy with tax breaks. President Bush and Congress agreed, and $152 billion was distributed to Americans through tax breaks. But the bad news kept coming.

Major investment banks, including Bear Stearns and Lehman Brothers, had invested heavily in stocks made up of the unsafe mortgages. Now that these stocks were worthless, the banks themselves were in danger of collapsing. It was the worst financial crisis since 1929, when the Wall Street crash had set off the Great Depression of the 1930s.

To prevent a second Wall Street crash, Paulson told President Bush in March, the U.S. government would have to bail out the banks. This advice went against the grain for George Bush. As a conservative Republican, he believed that the government should not interfere with the workings of the free market. Businesses that failed should be allowed to go out of business.

However, Bush did not want to go down in history as a second President Herbert Hoover. Hoover had taken office in 1929, at the onset of the Great Depression, and his policies were blamed for making the Depression worse. Bush agreed to support a rescue of Bear Stearns, hoping it would not be necessary for the government to step in again. He knew the bailout would not be a popular decision.

Sure enough, U.S. taxpayers were outraged that their hard-earned money was used to rescue a reckless bank. They blamed President Bush and his administration for not seeing the financial crisis coming and preventing it. By April 2008, 69 percent of Americans disapproved of Bush's performance. This made him the most unpopular president since Gallup began taking polls in the 1930s.

In May, George Bush took a brief break from the troubles of the country and the world to celebrate his daughter

Jenna's wedding. Jenna was marrying Henry Hager, a former assistant to Bush's political advisor Karl Rove. The private wedding ceremony, with only family and friends, took place at the Bush ranch in Crawford, Texas. George had tears in his eyes as he walked his daughter down the aisle. He usually went to bed early, but that night he stayed up until 1:00 A.M.

That summer the Olympic Games were held in Beijing, China, and George Bush, along with many other world leaders, attended. Although the spirit of the Olympic Games is supposed to be one of international friendship, the Russian prime minister, Vladimir Putin, chose this time to send troops into the neighboring Republic of Georgia. George Bush sat down next to Putin at the opening ceremony of the games and tried to tell him that he was making a serious mistake.

Putin calmly argued that Russia was only protecting the Russians who lived in Georgian territory from the Georgian "war criminals." It was clear that he had no intention of considering Bush's advice. Bush called him "cold-blooded" to his face.

Back home in Washington, President Bush and his advisors debated how to respond to Russia's aggression. They were concerned that if Russia succeeded in overturning the democratically elected government of Georgia, they would then feel free to invade other territories, such as the Crimea in Ukraine. But the United States was already fighting wars in Afghanistan and Iraq. Even Vice President Cheney agreed that responding to Russia with military force would be a mistake.

Meanwhile, the race for the 2008 presidency had narrowed down to Republican John McCain against Democrat Barack Obama. Barack Obama's campaign was telling voters that McCain as the next president would be "George W. Bush's third term." As for McCain, he was campaigning by blaming the Bush administration for the struggling economy. He also accused Bush of a "terribly mishandled" war in Iraq and a "disgraceful" response to the emergency of Hurricane Katrina. To Bush's disappointment, the McCain team thought it would not be helpful for the president to campaign for McCain or to attend the Republican National Convention at the end of August.

President Bush understood that it might be politically smart of McCain to keep his distance from Bush. However, he still insisted on appearing at the Republican convention, and he was scheduled to give a short speech on the first day. But the first day of the convention had to be canceled because of a hurricane. In the end, Bush gave his speech to the convention by video.

George Bush was impressed that the Democratic candidate had turned out to be Barack Obama. Bush was skeptical that Obama had the experience necessary to govern the country, but he thought the nomination of an African-American by a major party was a big step forward for racial equality. However, he remarked to an aide, "Whoever steps into this office, whether it's Obama or McCain, they're going to learn there's a big difference between campaigning and governing."

CHAPTER 21

"HISTORY WILL JUDGE"

GOVERNING THE UNITED STATES DURING THE FALL of 2008, President Bush began to feel like "the captain of a sinking ship." One after the other, major financial institutions threatened to fail and bring down the economy with them.

Lehman Brothers, an investment bank giant, actually did fail. The government seized control of the home mortgage companies Fannie Mae and Freddie Mac before they could collapse. The government bailed out the investment banks Merrill Lynch, Goldman Sachs, and Morgan Stanley. They bailed out AIG, a conglomerate that insured financial institutions.

Even so, the U.S. economy still teetered on the edge of disaster. President Bush and his advisors concluded that they would have to take sweeping action in order to head off a second Great Depression. At the end of September the Bush administration asked Congress to approve spending $700 billion on the Troubled Asset Relief Program (TARP). Congress resisted, knowing how angry voters would be if Congress spent still more money helping the banks that had caused the crisis in the first place. And many conservative Republicans still could not admit that the government needed to interfere with the free market.

But the day Congress voted against TARP, the stock market plummeted. The Dow Jones stock index lost 777 points. That was the largest one-day drop ever—even larger than on Black Tuesday in 1929. Secretary of the Treasury Paulson told President Bush, "This could be worse than 9/11 if we don't do something." Congress got the message, and a few days later both the Senate and the House had passed the TARP bill and the president had signed it.

Watching the last month of the presidential election campaign, George Bush thought that Senator Obama had a slight edge over John McCain. What voters cared most about was the economic crisis, and they believed that Obama would handle it better than McCain. Even moderate Republicans were leaning toward voting for the Democratic candidate.

Bush's former secretary of state, the widely respected Colin Powell, publicly endorsed Barack Obama.

On November 4, 2008, Barack Obama won by an overwhelming majority of electoral votes. George W. Bush was always a fierce competitor, and he was disappointed that his team—the Republican Party—had lost. Still, he was deeply moved that the United States had elected its first African-American president.

When the results of the election of 2008 were in, George Bush called Barack Obama and congratulated the president-elect. He invited Obama to visit the White House so they could discuss what awaited the new administration. President Bush and his team had already been planning to make the transition as smooth as possible.

On November 10, George and Laura Bush welcomed Barack and Michelle Obama to the White House. Bush and Obama sat down together in the president's Oval Office, and President Bush explained the preparations his administration had drawn up. His main concern for the new president was security, in case the Obama team faced an emergency right after his inauguration. Bush and his advisors had thought about how to handle the worst scenarios they could imagine: What if North Korea launched a nuclear weapon? What if enemy hackers sabotaged U.S. computer systems?

Bush also briefed Obama on the continuing economic crisis. Now the major American automakers, General Motors, Ford, and Chrysler, were on the point of collapse. Like the banks, the auto giants were in trouble through their own mismanagement. The popular view was that they deserved to fail.

Yet if the government didn't bail them out, hundreds of thousands of American workers would lose their jobs—a terrible blow to the already weak economy. Through TARP, Bush planned to give the auto industry enough money to last through March. Then it would be up to the Obama administration.

In December, George Bush made one last trip to Iraq. He had worked out a plan with Prime Minister Nouri al-Maliki for ending the war, and now, in a hopeful, upbeat mood, they would sign the agreement. But at the press conference before, the good feeling was shattered by an Iraqi journalist in the audience. Pulling off his shoes, he hurled them at the American president.

Luckily, Bush had quick reflexes, and he ducked one shoe after the other. He assured the Secret Service agents protecting him that he was okay. But Maliki and the other Iraqis were horrified. In the Arab world, throwing a shoe at someone is a deadly insult.

Bush did his best to calm everyone down. He joked to the press, "If you want the facts, it's a size-10 shoe that he threw." He went on with the signing and the following banquet. However, the incident was a low note on which to end his long and difficult relationship with Iraq.

On January 19, 2009, the day before Barack Obama's inauguration, George Bush made farewell calls to several world leaders. One of them was Vladimir Putin. Bush still thought of the Russian prime minister as a friend, in spite of the fact that Putin didn't seem to get the concept of democracy. Back in 2006 Putin had suggested to Bush that he should go for a third term as president of the United States, in order to prevent the next president from changing his policies.

Putin knew that the U.S. Constitution limited the president to two terms. But he thought that Bush could easily get around that rule: just change the constitution. The Russian constitution banned more than two *consecutive* terms, and Putin did leave the presidency in 2008, but only to take up another high office, as prime minister, for the next four years. In addition he would have the law changed so that beginning in 2012, the president would serve for six years instead of four. Putin himself would be that president, elected for a third term.

The next day George W. Bush stood by on the Capitol steps as Barack Obama took the oath of president of the United States. Then the new president escorted the former president through the Capitol to Marine One, and Bush climbed aboard the presidential helicopter for the last time. "Come on, Laura," he said to the former First Lady, "we're going home." During the ride to Andrews Air Force Base, Bush's aides noticed that he seemed to relax. They could almost see the burdens of the presidency drop from his shoulders, for the first time in eight years

The Bushes flew to Midland, Texas, where George W. Bush spoke to a rally of thousands of cheering fans. From Midland, George and Laura flew on to Crawford, and the peace and quiet of their ranch. Bush had to remind himself that the relentless schedule he had followed as president was over. As he described it, "I felt like I had gone from a hundred miles an hour to about ten."

George had made a point of keeping fit during his stressful years as president, and he was still fit and healthy when he left the office at age sixty-two. In his new life, he announced, he planned to improve his golf game. But he also had serious goals. He wrote a second memoir, *Decision Points,* published in 2010, which told the story of his eight years in the White House from his point of view.

Another way Bush planned to preserve a record of his presidency was to complete the George W. Bush Presidential Center at Southern Methodist University in Dallas. The center was officially opened in April 2013, with President Barack Obama and former presidents Bill Clinton, Jimmy Carter, and George H. W. Bush attending the dedication. Bush joked to the audience, "There was a time in my life when I wasn't likely to be found *in* a library, much less found one."

George W. Bush was especially glad that his father could be present at the ceremony, although George H. W. Bush, now eighty-eight, was in a wheelchair. Bush felt lucky to be the only former president whose parents were still alive. And his first grandchild, Jenna and Henry's daughter, Margaret Laura Hager, had just been born on April 13.

George and Laura Bush moved into a new home in

Dallas, where they expected to live as private citizens. But ex-presidents never really regain the privacy they had before the White House. So many sightseers drove down their street, just to peer at the Bushes' house, that a gate had to be installed across the roadway.

During the White House years, the staff had done everything for the Bushes, from bringing morning coffee to walking Barney, their Scottish terrier. Now it was George who made coffee for Laura and himself in the morning, and George who walked Barney around the neighborhood. He thought it was a good joke that he, former leader of the most powerful nation in the world, was now picking up after a dog.

However, former presidents still have influence they can use for good causes. When a major earthquake shook the poverty-stricken Caribbean nation of Haiti in 2010, President Obama called George Bush and Bill Clinton to the White House. He asked them to team up and lead the American relief effort for Haiti.

Bush and Clinton were longtime political opponents, but personally they got along well. During his presidency, George had felt free to call Bill and complain about how hard it was to get Congress to cooperate. Now George and

Bill's joint fund raised millions of dollars to help Haitians recover from the disaster.

A project especially dear to George Bush's heart was the President's Emergency Plan for AIDS Relief (PEPFAR), an AIDS relief program he had launched in Africa in 2003. The program provided antiretroviral drugs for people suffering from AIDS, as well as care for children whose parents had died from the disease. PEPFAR was the largest initiative in all of history for fighting a single disease, and it succeeded in saving millions of African lives.

In the last year of Bush's presidency, he had extended the program for another five years and another $48 billion. That same year, 2008, he and Laura had visited several countries in Africa. Everywhere they went, crowds of grateful people turned out to cheer them. It was one of George Bush's happiest moments as president. He was glad to know that PEPFAR would continue to save lives after he left the White House. In 2013 George and Laura visited Zambia and took part in renovating a cervical cancer clinic. This project was part of the global health initiative included in the George W. Bush Institute.

Another favorite cause of George's was supporting and honoring military veterans, so the George W. Bush

Institute also included a military service initiative. One of the initiative's yearly events was the "wounded warrior" hundred-kilometer mountain bike ride. Every year, beginning in 2011, George Bush was happy to pedal the course with some twenty veterans wounded in service since 2001.

As a former president, Bush kept his distance from American politics. During the presidential race of 2012, when Republican Mitt Romney challenged Barack Obama, Bush did not campaign for Romney. When he was asked by reporters, he simply stated, "I'm for Mitt Romney" and "Mitt Romney is going to be a great president." Likewise, Bush refused to comment publicly on the actions of the Obama administration. As he explained to late-night TV host Jay Leno, "I don't think it's good for the country to have a former president criticize his successor."

George Bush did give one opinion about President Obama, when Obama was criticized for playing golf. "I think he ought to play golf. To be able to get outside and play golf with some of your pals is important for the president. It does give you an outlet."

Unexpectedly, George Bush took up painting as a new hobby for his "afterlife," as Laura called the post-presidency. He worked seriously at learning to paint, taking weekly lessons and painting every day. He signed the pictures with "43," because he was the forty-third president.

In the spring of 2014 George Bush exhibited a collection of portraits he had painted of world leaders, including Vladimir Putin and Tony Blair, former prime minister of Britain. "I'm not a great painter," he said, and most art critics agreed. However, many thought these portraits succeeded in expressing George Bush's personal impression of each leader. The portrait of Putin, looking "cold-blooded," as George had called him, was especially commented on.

George W. Bush often seemed to be having fun these days, as in a video of him participating in a fund-raising drive for the disease ALS (known as Lou Gehrig's disease). The idea of the fund-raiser was to have a bucket of ice water dumped on him. But he explained with a straight face, "I do not think it's presidential for me to be splashed with ice water, so I'm simply going to write you a check." As he began to write, Laura Bush gleefully dumped a bucket of ice water over his head.

George W. Bush had always thought of his father as a hero. In 2014 he published a book about him, *41: A Portrait of My Father,* that expressed his admiration and love for George H. W. Bush. He believed that his father had not been fairly appreciated as president. This book, he hoped, would help more Americans realize that the forty-first president had done a good job, after all.

As for George W. Bush's own presidency, he knew that he had not achieved many of his goals. The war in Iraq had consumed his second term. By early 2009 the war had cost the United States over $600 billion, and thousands of Americans had lost their lives fighting in Iraq.

The Iraq War had crippled Bush's attempts to reform Social Security, the tax code, and immigration policy. He had hoped to encourage a more cooperative spirit between Republicans and Democrats, but instead the war had further divided Americans. And the war had distracted the Bush administration from the oncoming Great Recession until it was almost too late.

During his eight-year presidency, George Bush had gradually become concerned about the threat of world climate change. He tried to encourage the development of alternative sources of energy, and in his last year in office, he made attempts to get power plants to reduce their emissions of greenhouse gases. But by then President Bush had lost much of his political clout. And Americans were too worried about losing their jobs, houses, and retirement savings to focus on longer-term threats.

However, George W. Bush was proud that in his second term he had fulfilled his most important charge as president: keeping the United States safe from attacks. The U.S. economy was still in deep trouble, but at least the TARP plan had prevented another Great Depression. In Iraq the war was not over, but at least the surge in U.S. troops had kept the country from collapsing into civil war. And he had done what he could to advance the cause of freedom in the world.

In the years after George Bush left office, his approval ratings in public opinion polls rose steadily. However, Bush knew it was too soon to judge how well he had met the many challenges, foreseen as well as unforeseen, of the presidency. Looking back on his important decisions, he himself thought that some of them had been right, and some had been wrong. He believed he had done his best. In the end, he said, "I did what I did and ultimately history will judge."

TIME LINE

July 6, 1946: George Walker Bush is born in New Haven, Connecticut.

1948: Bush family moves to Texas, where George spends his childhood in Midland and Houston.

1964: GWB graduates from Phillips Academy, a boarding school in Andover, Massachusetts.

1968: GWB graduates from Yale University, with a BS in history. He serves in the Texas Air National Guard as a fighter pilot until 1973.

1975: GWB graduates from Harvard Business School with a master's degree in business administration.

1975: GWB moves back to Midland, Texas, where he begins a career in the oil industry.

1976: George H. W. Bush, father of George W. Bush, becomes director of the CIA (Central Intelligence Agency).

November 5, 1977: GWB marries Laura Welch.

November 25, 1981: Twin daughters, Barbara and Jenna, are born to Laura and GWB.

November 1988: George H. W. Bush is elected forty-first president of the United States.

April 1989: GWB and investment partners arrange the purchase of the Texas Rangers baseball team.

November 1994: GWB is elected governor of Texas, defeating incumbent Ann Richards.

November 1998: GWB is reelected governor of Texas. Jeb Bush, GWB's younger brother, is elected governor of Florida.

December 13, 2000: GWB and Vice President Dick Cheney are declared winners of the presidential election over Democrats Albert Gore and Joseph Lieberman.

January 20, 2001: GWB is inaugurated as the forty-third president of the United States.

September 11, 2001: Terrorists attack the World Trade Center in New York City and the Pentagon in Washington, D.C., and hijack another plane that ultimately crashes into the Western Pennsylvania countryside.

October 7, 2001: In response to the 9/11 terrorist attacks, the United States launches Operation Enduring Freedom and goes to war against Taliban targets in Afghanistan.

January 8, 2002: GWB signs the No Child Left Behind Act for education reform.

March 19, 2003: GWB signs an executive order for the first U.S. strikes on Baghdad, Iraq.

2003: GWB signs the HIV/AIDS Act and the Jobs and Growth Tax Relief Reconciliation Act.

2004: GWB and Vice President Dick Cheney win reelection in November over Democrats John F. Kerry and John Edwards. U.S. Secretary of State Colin Powell resigns.

January 20, 2005: GWB sworn in for second term.

January 2005: Dr. Condoleezza Rice becomes U.S. secretary of state.

August 29, 2005: Hurricane Katrina, the third strongest hurricane ever recorded to make landfall in the United States, strikes the Gulf Coast.

TIME LINE

2006: Saddam Hussein is found guilty of war crimes and is put to death in Iraq.

2006: Dr. Robert Gates replaces Donald Rumsfeld as secretary of defense.

2008: GWB signs the Emergency Economic Stabilization Act. He issues a $17.4 billion auto bailout to General Motors and Chrysler to keep the companies from going bankrupt.

January 20, 2009: GWB and Laura attend President Barack Obama's inauguration. Following the ceremony, they fly to Midland, Texas, where a crowd of nearly twenty thousand welcomes them home.

SOURCES

BOOKS

Baker, Peter. *Days of Fire: Bush and Cheney in the White House.* New York: Doubleday, 2013.

Bush, Barbara. *Barbara Bush: A Memoir.* New York: Scribner, 1994.

Bush, George H.W. *All the Best, George Bush: My Life in Letters and Other Writings.* New York: Scribner, 1999.

Bush, George W. *Decision Points.* New York: Crown Publishers, 2010.

Bush, George W., and Karen Hughes. *A Charge to Keep.* New York: Morrow, 1999.

Bush, Laura. *Spoken from the Heart.* New York: Scribner, 2010.

Horne, Jed. *Breach of Faith: Hurricane Katrina and the Near Death of a Great American City.* New York: Random House, 2006.

Minutaglio, Bill. *First Son: George W. Bush and the Bush Family Dynasty.* New York: Random House, 1999.

Mitchell, Elizabeth. *Revenge of the Bush Dynasty.* New York: Hyperion, 2000.

Parnet, Herbert. *George Bush: The Life of a Lone Star Yankee.* New York: Scribner, 1997.

MAGAZINES AND NEWSPAPERS

Baker, Peter. "Bush (43) Shares Spotlight With Bush (41) as Tribute Book Is Published." *New York Times,* November 12, 2014, A15.

Bruni, Frank. "Loyalty Prized Above All in Heart of Bush Country." *New York Times,* July 20, 2000.

Bush, Laura. "Excerpts from Laura Bush's Speech to the G.O.P. Convention." *New York Times,* August 1, 2000.

SOURCES

Christie, Les. "California cities fill top 10 foreclosure list." CNNMoney.com, August 14, 2007.

Hennessy-Fiske, Molly. "At George W. Bush Library, five presidents meet in harmony." *The Los Angeles Times*, April 25, 2013.

Kristof, Nicholas D. "Ally of an Older Generation amid the Tumult of the Sixties." *New York Times,* June 19, 2000.

———. "A Philosophy with Roots in Conservative Texas Soil." *New York Times,* May 21, 2000.

———. "Bush's Choice in War: Devoid of Passion or Anxiety." *New York Times,* July 11, 2000.

———. "Earning A's in People Skills at Andover." *New York Times,* June 10, 2000.

Lemann, Nicholas. "The Redemption." *New Yorker,* January 31, 2000.

Myerson, Harold. "The Case for Keeping Big Three Out of Bankruptcy." *American Prospect*, November 24, 2008.

Romano, Lois. "Inner Circle Provides Humor, Strength and a Fierce Loyalty." *Washington Post,* July 26, 2000.

Thomas, Jo. "After Yale, Bush Ambled Amiably into His Future." *New York Times*, July 22, 2000.

Trejos, Nancy. "Existing-Homes Sales Fall Steeply." *Washington Post,* April 25, 2007.

Viser, Matt. "Activity links commanders in chief." *Boston Globe*, August 8, 2014.

INTERNET

Bryant, Nick. "George W Bush exhibits his paintings of world leaders." http://web.archive.org/web/20140405084128/http://www.bbc.com/news/world-us-canada-26890910

Bush, George W. Second Inaugural Speech. http://georgewbush-whitehouse.archives.gov/news/releases/2005/01/20050120-1.html

237

SOURCES

Gerson, Michael. "Looking back on a decade of PEPFAR." http://www
.one.org/us/2014/07/01/michael-gerson-looking-back-on-a-decade
-of-pepfar/

Jackson, David, "G.W. Bush: Romney will make 'great' president." http://
www.usatoday.com/story/theoval/2012/10/16/george-w-bush-mitt
-romney-barack-obama-election-2012/1636227/

Loinez, Alexis L. "George W. Bush gushes about granddaughter on the
Tonight Show." http://www.people.com/people/article/0,,20757874,00
.html

Reiff, Laura Foote. "The Winds of Immigration Reform Blow Again."
http://www.natlawreview.com/article/winds-immigration-reform
-blow-again-part-1

"Bush Accepts Sen. McCain's Torture Policy." http://www.nbcnews.com
/id/10480690/#.VCmrJunu2M8

"Hurricane Katrina (12L) Approaching the Gulf Coast."
http://visibleearth.nasa.gov/view.php?id=74693
http://georgewbush-whitehouse.archives.gov/reports/katrina-lessons
-learned/chapter4.html

"Poll: Bush Ratings at All-Time Low." http://www.cbsnews.com/news
/poll-bush-ratings-at-all-time-low/

"Thousands Join Anti-War Protest." http://news.bbc.co.uk/2/hi/uk
_news/england/london/4818952.stm

United States Department of Labor, Bureau of Labor Statistics. http://
data.bls.gov/timeseries/LNU04032231?data_tool=XGtable

"What Caused McCain's Poll Numbers to Fall?" http://www.latimes.com
/la-oew-schnur-cain3-2008nov03-story.html#page=1

"George W. Bush becomes a grandpa." http://www.usatoday.com
/story/news/politics/2013/04/14/jenna-bush-mila-bush-george-w
-bush/2082381/

"The Clinton Bush Haiti Fund Commits Its Remaining Funds." http://
www.clintonbushhaitifund.org/news/entry/the-clinton-bush-haiti
-fund-commits-its-remaining-funds/

238

SOURCES

"George W. Bush takes ice bucket challenge." http://www.today.com/video/today/55901869

"George W. Bush: 'History Will Judge.'" http://www.politico.com/story/2013/04/george-w-bush-usa-today-interview-presidential-library-90417.html

VIDEO

"George W. Bush." *Biography.* A&E Television Networks, 1996.

INDEX

INDEX

241

INDEX

242

INDEX

243

INDEX

244

INDEX

INDEX